REGIONALISM
AND WORLD ORDER

REGIONALISM AND WORLD ORDER

By RONALD J. YALEM

University of Southern California

Public Affairs Press, Washington, D. C.

TO SUNNY AND GARY

FOREWORD

A fundamental problem confronting social scientists who study the structures and processes of the international system is to learn how that system may be controlled. This is an important question when it is approached in a nationalist perspective. From this standpoint, the need is to know how the relations between nations can be ordered and directed to serve best the interests of security and welfare of one's own country. From an internationalist point of view, the issue of control is not less a crucial consideration because world order, bearing its ultimate fruits of security, protection, progress, and well-being for all peoples and countries, can be regarded no longer as the forthcoming result of historical evolution. Instead, the twentieth century experiences with international relations have undermined thoroughly the optimistic faith in the inevitable progress of human affairs and have replaced that faith with a conviction that, if the relations of nations continue to run along their "natural" routes as they have always done in history, the prospect is for a tremendous disaster in store sometimes before the end of the century.

The fact of a vastly increased capability of destruction across national boundaries is the new variable in the situation and there is no firm basis for the assumption that this capability would not be used to the hilt at the moment that the requirements and circumstances of international politics call for its use. Hence, the "natural" performance of the international system must be modified by purposeful intervention and its usual sequences, known well in history, must be interrupted. From these observations come the contentions that individual national states cannot, any longer, preserve themselves by their own devices, that national and international interests have become identical, at the root, and that the means of control and the will to control the international system for the purposes of general security and welfare have become paramount requirements.

Professor Yalem addresses himself in this book to one sector of the stubborn and difficult problem of control in the international system. Although it is not the only conceivable means of governing the affairs among nations, the development of international organizations has

v

NOV 4 - 1965

long since been seen as the most likely method of interrupting traditional international practices and replacing them with new and better
approaches to world order.

The stupendous difficulty faced in trying to raise the structure of an
effective *universal* international organization—we remain in 1965
disconcertingly close to 1919 in this matter—has stimulated a partially alternative strategy of attempting to build piecemeal, multiple,
and diverse *regional* international organizations. In this book will be
found an analysis and assessment of the interplay of forces, ideas, and
influences which have reciprocated and reverberated during the
twentieth century in the relations of the unreconstructed international
system with the advent of univesal international organizations and the
rise of regional international organizations.

To take a close look at this complex picture in its historical setting
and to arrive at the tentative but firm conclusion that things are not,
in fact, going well either in the dovetailing of regional functions and
structures with the universal organization movement or in the progress
toward international control of the system of relations of national
states are not the processes which raise hopes or win the plaudits of
the crowd. Yet, it is only the ceaseless analysis and evaluation of
how things stand, in fact, and not as we wished they were, that is
likely to bring about forward motion toward world order and a controlled international environment. The need may have never been
greater in international affairs for plans, inspirations, blueprints, and
Utopian pictures of the world as it could be but it is also imperative
that these designs be anchored at one end to the real situations of the
immediate past and present.

By focusing attention on the record and the role of regional organizations and their relationship with the problem of world order, Professor
Yalem has made a substantial contribution to the understanding of the
anchored end of the existing and real situation. He has carried out
this useful work with commendable modesty and critical skill. He
offers no absolute answers but he raises the right questions. As he
points out repeatedly, the future of international organizations in a
time of great transformations of the international system will require
constant scholarly attention and increasingly refined and competent
analyses.

CHARLES A. McCLELLAND

CONTENTS

CONTENTS

CHAPTER I

INTRODUCTION

The striking proliferation of regional organizations since 1945 is one of the most significant developments of contemporary international relations. Such a growth was not envisioned by the framers of the United Nations Charter who believed that regionalism must be subordinated to the universal approach to peace and security. What is the relationship between such organizations and the United Nations? Is regionalism a symptom or a cause of international disorder? Assuming the continued growth of regional organizations, how will this affect the possibilities of promoting world order? If both regional and universal approaches continue to be utilized, what are the most workable relationships—legal, administrative, and political—between them? Finally, do regional organizations in particular and does regionalism in general represent a movement away from exclusive reliance on the nation-state as the basic unit of international relations?

The purpose of this study is to examine and suggest tentative conclusions to these questions by exploring the theoretical assumptions of regionalism and examining them on the basis of the historical development of regional and universal international organizations since 1920. The influence of international political factors on international organization will be described and analyzed. While the central focus is on the extent to which regionalism affects world order, it is hoped that the study will also reveal the extent to which regionalism is a reaction to international disorder.

World order is conceived as an ideal condition of the international system of sovereign states in which relations between states are governed on the basis of law and noncoercive procedures rather than power politics and force. It is postulated that movement toward this ideal demands a reinforcing equilibrium between universal and regional organizations; the exclusion of either form of international cooperation is considered unrealistic. A world order based on regional organizations alone is apt to be a recrudescence of the regional balance-of-power politics that preceded and precipitated the first world conflict of the twentieth century. Similarly, universalism as a base for world order is incomplete without recognition that

1

despite the fact that science and technology have reduced the significance of geographic distance, regional cooperation is an increasingly important phenomenon of international life.

It may be useful to differentiate between a normative concept of world order based upon minimization, but not elimination, of power politics through the primacy of universal organization and the prevailing condition of international disorder in which power politics and regionalism are dominant forces. Throughout the study numerous references to the balance of power are presented as evidence of the gap between world order as a normative condition of the international system and the actual contemporary pattern of power politics. In no way do these frequent allusions to the balance of power diminish the author's belief in the desirability of attaining the normative condition; they simply reflect his honest observation of the real condition of the international system.

Perhaps the discrepancy is most discernible with regard to the theory and practice of collective security. As a theory it envisions the entire community of nations poised to initiate military action against any aggressor on an immediate and unconditional basis. Yet rarely has the unity of purpose necessary to sustain such action been found practical. Instead states have concluded regional alliances based on homogeneity of interests and mobilized not for universal action but for selective security of some for some, rather than all for all. [1] The distinction is important because of the tendency of statesmen to assert that regional systems are intended to provide collective security; this is a fiction, because the theory of collective security presupposes universal effort and impartial action against any aggressor—conditions lacking in regional security arrangements.

This study was undertaken on the basis of a conviction that a fuller analysis and evaluation of the relationship between regional and universal approaches to world order is needed to clarify an increasingly important problem of contemporary international relations: the nature of the continuing disequilibrium between universal and regional international organization and its implications. The methods utilized are historical and analytical rather than descriptive. Many excellent studies of individual universal and regional agencies are readily available, and while it is difficult to make analytical assessments without reference to the descriptive feature of such agencies, relevant information will be introduced to preserve the overall analytical focus of the study.

The related problem of identifying and considering the factors responsible for expanding the process of regional integration is surveyed on the basis of the experience of Western Europe. Fuller treatment of the integration process may be desirable but is precluded by the paucity of research in this field. Although the nature of regional bloc politics in the United Nations is an interesting byproduct of the regionalization of world politics, it is omitted from this study. The author justifies this omission on the grounds that this phenomenon does not significantly affect the equilibrium or diequilibrium between universal and regional organizations.

Initial Assumptions. To be meaningful a serious study of the interaction of universal and regional organization requires the stipulation of certain tentative assumptions. The enumeration of a number of basic assumptions serves to sharpen the analytical focus and to delimit the scope of the phenomena to be examined. It is indispensable as a background for understanding the theoretical and empirical data which forms the main body of the study. Verification of these assumptions, however, must await the accumulation of additional evidence. This is so because positive confirmation is difficult when one is analyzing so complex and dynamic a relationship as that occurring between universalism and regionalism, and also because of the relatively short time period in which these two forms of interstate cooperation have functioned. Following are the initial assumptions upon which this study has been based:

(1) The proliferation of regional security agencies since 1945 constitutes an organizational and political response to changes in the structure of the balance of power and the emergence of sharply conflicting ideological systems rather than a deliberate attempt to establish such agencies on the basis of their theoretical advantages over universal cooperation.

(2) Universal and regional forms of international cooperation are inseparable in theory and cannot be viewed as alternatives but as theoretically compatible and mutually supporting. Empirical observation, however, often discloses that this theoretical conjointment is vitiated by the influence of disintegrative factors that bring about a disequilibrium and practical incompatibility.

(3) While regional cooperation is affected by the global balance of power, changes in weapons technology, and especially by the appearance of an external threat to regional security, it is also influenced

by certain intra-regional factors that may accelerate or retard the process of regional integration. An underlying cultural, economic, and political solidarity may be indispensable for the success of regional cooperation, but it is not self-sufficient. Successful regional cooperation is the product of a complex interaction of regional homogeneity and its tangible expression in regional institutions. Expanding integration is a reflection of an underlying regional solidarity enhanced by institutional collaboration.

(4) Within the six-nation area encompassed by the European Economic Community and sister organizations, traditional cooperation is being replaced by new patterns of supranational cooperation and interdependence that may culminate in the establishment of a regional federation or confederation. If the nation-state is in retreat in this area, there are no indications that a similar process is under way in any of the non-Western regions which are too fragmented by goals of national self-sufficiency and political instability.

(5) The multiplication of regional security agencies since 1945 presents serious implications especially with regard to the impact of such organizations on the quest for international peace and security. The evidence does not suggest that these agencies have improved the prospects for peace or security. Though they were established for this purpose, regional security agencies are primarily a symptom of the rapid deterioration of international order after 1945. At the same time acting independently of the weakened universal organization and unrestrained by any "balancer" actor, they have also exacerbated international tensions.

(6) While in the real world of international politics the tension between universalism and regionalism is sharpest in the field of peace and security, some interaction may be perceived between universal and regional welfare organizations. In this area the problem is less a usurpation by regional agencies of responsibility for functional activities than the costly and duplicative operations of universal agencies themselves and the lack of coordination between such agencies and regional functionalist organizations.

(7) The future relationship between universal and regional organizations cannot be predicted, but a modest statement of probable trends is impossible without an examination of the influence of nuclear weapons on the structure of the balance of power. The diffusion of such weapons to non-Western states or blocs in the distant future may induce a change from bipolarity to multipolarity, but the emer-

gence of a multi-bloc international system is apt to only accentuate rather than reverse the contemporary disequilibrium favoring regionalism.

(8) The contemporary disequilibrium between universalism and regionalism is unlikely to be reversed unless the two superpowers can agree on a permanent ideological accommodation to be followed by agreement to refuse to disperse nuclear weapons to third powers. Dispersal of such weapons would not only endanger international peace by increasing the numerical possibility of nuclear attack, but would hamper the possible reintegration of non-Western regional blocs into the United Nations system.

The foregoing assumptions on which this study is based have been derived from an extensive empirical examination of the major scholarly sources devoted to regionalism as a significant phenomenon of contemporary international relations. The empirical findings are presented in Chapters III through VIII. Insofar as the theoretical aspects of regionalism are concerned, Chapter II constitutes an exposition of various theories of regionalism. Consequently, the relationship between the initial assumptions and such theories is largely to sharpen for the reader the distance between regionalism in theory and regionalism in practice.

THEORIES OF REGIONALISM

Crucial to an understanding of the problem of regionalism and world order is an examination of its theoretical basis. In this chapter we will consider a number of theories of regionalism that attempt to explain the nature of regional cooperation, the elements or preconditions for such cooperation, and the internal and external factors that influence the dynamics of regionalism. This theoretical background will serve as a basis for an assessment of regionalism and world order in terms of the actual performance of regional organizations described in subsequent chapters.

While political theory often serves as a rationalization subsequent to the development of institutional forms and structures, it may also serve as a guide to political action. And if a new institution departs from the model upon which it was based, this departure provides empirical evidence from which the scholar may seek to confirm various theoretical propositions. For example, the theory of a world community united to suppress aggression through collective sanctions action proved incapable of practical fulfillment under the League of Nations and was only partially implemented under the United Nations. On the basis of the disparity between legal norms and political realities we may better perceive the limitations of the universalist approach to world order.

Similarly, the failure of regional organizations to coalesce as the embryonic foundations of a universal order is a refutation of an important aspect of regional theory. On the other hand, the experience of universal and regional organizations does confirm the general theoretical proposition that individual nation-states may cooperate through institutional arrangements to solve common problems.

Various theoretical aspects of the regionalist approach to international cooperation will now be examined. Although it has been asserted that a proper balance between universalism and regionalism cannot be attained on the basis of theory, practical developments in the field of international organization are often justified in terms of theory however much the institutions created may alter under the influence of international politics.[1]

Among scholars of regionalism there appears to be a wide consensus on the basic advantages of regional as opposed to universal cooperation: geographic proximity is more likely to promote cooperation than geographic separateness; states located within a particular region are better able to cooperate because of greater cultural, social, and political homogeneity. [2]

Thus, Professor I. L. Claude finds that "regionalism is sometimes put forward as an alternative to globalism, a superior substitute for the principle of universality . . ." on the grounds ". . . that only within limited segments of the globe can we find the cultural foundations of common loyalties, the objective similarity of national problems, and the potential awareness of common interests which are necessary for the effective functioning of multilateral institutions." [3]

Similarly, Professor Pitman Potter asserts that "the basic idea of the regionalist is that the conditions obtaining in any particular area . . . tend to give the nations located there a certain community of interest" which leads to "a distinct and separate international organization." [4]

Sometimes the supposed advantages of regionalism are used to explain the reasons for its growth. In accounting for the rapid development of regionalism since 1945, Professor Norman Padelford suggested that in addition to geographical proximity, regional cooperation may be fostered because of security considerations; to stimulate economic development; to provide a framework for the peaceful settlement of intra-regional disputes; and as a device for the promotion and stabilization of regional political equilibrium. [5] Regional groupings as diverse as the European Coal and Steel Community, the Arab League, the North Atlantic Treaty Organization, and the European Economic Community may be explained on the basis of one or more of the above factors.

Community solidarity as the basis of regionalism is emphasized by Professor Pierre Vellas who notes that while there may be a degree of cultural diversity among the units, "there must be some commonly held ideas, some cohesive spiritual forces within in addition to motivations of economic need, self-defense and security." [6]

In its eighth report the Commission to Study the Organization of Peace (hereafter referred to as the Commission) advanced several arguments in support of regional cooperation as an adjunct rather than a substitute for universal cooperation. These arguments centered on the value of regional organizations in promoting regional

security and the pacific settlement of disputes, providing more equitable means of representation for small states, and in facilitating a
stable balance of power. [7] The following analysis explores these
arguments as a preliminary introduction to the problem of the relationship between universalism and regionalism.

Regional cooperation has often been justified on the assumption
that the defense and security of a geographic region is easier to
establish on the regional rather than the universal level. Advocates
of regionalism assert that "defense . . . is necessarily regional, even
with modern weapons of war. . . ." requiring the "preparation of
bases, materials and formations against the most probable source of
aggression . . ."[8] Defense and security planning is said to be
". . . only possible within a group of states commanding mutual
confidence and with a common interest in defense from the same
source of aggression." [9]

The regionalist approach to peace and security amounts to a denial
of the feasibility of the theory of universal collective security by
denying its major assumption the indivisibility of peace. Regionalists assume that the outbreak of aggression will be of direct concern
only to those states located within the area, and that extra-regional
states will not respond with assistance because their vital interests
are not threatened. As long as warfare remains localized this argument
has validity as demonstrated by the Korean conflict of 1950 in which
only 16 members of the United Nations participated. But when
conflict engulfs several regions, the vital interests of most states are
endangered and the viability of regional security arrangements is put
to the severest test.

The failure of collective security under the League of Nations and
its only limited success under the United Nations has reinforced regionalist arguments. Inability of the United Nations to guarantee
peace and security because of the Soviet-American split in the Security
Council has encouraged the formation of numerous regional military
alliances predicated on a more certain response to aggression. Whether
such groupings produce greater security for their members is questionable. The great defect of contemporary regionalism is the "political competition . . . [that] tends to daw states into a bi-polarized
world of great instability." [10]

Since 1945 the international political system has been bifurcated
by the intense competition of the rival blocs of the Soviet Union
and the United States, and the United Nations has been reduced

to impotence insofar as the control of such regional alliances are concerned. In defense of the United Nations, however, it should be recognized that the organization was not endowed with the power to mediate great power conflict and it is therefore incapable of taking punitive action against great power aggression. If the major premise of the United Nations has not been realized in the form of continual cooperation of the great powers to maintain peace, the fault lies not so much with the organization as with the emergence of a great power rivalry that was not anticipated when the United Nations was established. Under such circumstances, the flight from universalism to regionalism was not unnatural.

A second argument favoring regionalism is based on the alleged superiority of regional agencies in the pacific settlement of international disputes. Because of their greater degree of solidarity, regional agencies are able to adjust intraregional disputes. But this assumes that international disputes may be confined to regions whereas in fact the interests of states are increasingly extra-regional and may involve inter-regional conflicts that may more appropriately be considered by a universal agency. Furthermore, as will be discussed in a later chapter, regional agencies have not been conspicuously successful in solving intra-regional disputes.

The counter-argument to the alleged superiority of regionalism in the pacific settlement of disputes is that "within a universal organization it is possible to utilize the services of distant states with no political interest in a given dispute, for fact-finding, consultation or arbitration." [11] Unfortunately, in the contemporary bipolarized world there are very few disputes that can be isolated from the politics of great power rivalry thereby nullifying the utility of a universal agency to function in an impartial manner. Only in those disputes in which the vital interests of the great powers do not collide can the universal organization be effective. The record of the United Nations, however, reveals that even in such cases settlement is more likely to depend on the actions of the disputants than on the limited conciliation and mediation powers of the universal agency.

It has also been maintained that regionalism affords a more equitable system of representation for small states than is possible within a universal organization where such states often find it difficult to secure places on the major decision-making councils. [12] The tremendous expansion in the membership of the United Nations has reduced possibilities for the individual smaller nations to be elected

to nonpermanent membership on the Security Council or obtain seats
on the Economic and Social Council. In the General Assembly, however, the smaller states now command increasing strength with which
to mobilize support for their policies.

Although regional groupings may permit smaller states to secure
greater representation on decision-making councils, such states do not
necessarily gain prestige or power as a result of such membership.
The tendency seems to be established that regional associations fall
under the sway of one or more great powers located in the region. [13]

On the other hand, the requirement of unanimity on the decisions
of the NATO Council theoretically confers on the smaller members
of this coalition a right of veto as a check on the dominant power of
the United States. Though in practice such vetoes may rarely be
employed, an interesting example of the use of a veto is provided by
the practice of two international committees attached to NATO that
are charged with the responsibility for formulating strategic trade
controls toward Soviet bloc countries.[14] In a number of cases the United
States had had to defer to the wishes of the smaller states for periodic
relaxation of the restrictions on trade with Communist China and
the European Soviet bloc.[15]

Regional organizations have also often been advocated as solutions
to the problem of stabilizing the balance of power, especially through
the creation of multiple centers of power as an antidote to the contemporary bipolar system.[16]   A stable balance may be promoted
"as the independent units of power become more numerous,
as they become more equal, and as they become separated by de-
fensible geographic barriers.' [17]

Circumstances of the modern era, however, make such preconditions of stability unlikely because of the following factors: adequate
regional balancing is difficult to attain with the decline in the number
of independent and equal power centers while geographic barriers are
of lesser significance as a result of changing technology which permits
the launching of surprise attack through intercontinental ballistic
missiles.

Insofar as the regional as distinguished from the global balance
of power is concerned, it has been argued that "smaller states within
a region, by organizing as a unit, can often present adequate defense
against their large neighbors . . ." and thereby stabilize a regional
balance of power; yet the history of regional agencies does not provide much support for this thesis.[18] Any effectiveness of NATO

against the threat of Soviet imperialism in Western Europe depends upon the protective nuclear deterrent of the United States which far surpasses the total military power of the other fourteen members of the alliance. Much the same thing could be said about the other regional agencies in which the United States is involved such as the Organization of American States and the Southeast Asia Treaty Organization. Regional organizations therefore can only be effective as security systems unless they are protected by a great power, thereby indicating differences in strength between the smaller members and the great power.

The danger of this disequilibrium is that the smaller states trade one kind of insecurity for another. That is, they may find that their exposed position outside of a regional security system is less objectionable than their military inferiority within a great power orbit which often leads to a *de facto* loss of independence in exchange for the protection afforded by the great power. This has long been a major complaint by the smaller members of NATO with regard to the United States. Within the inter-American system the military weakness of the twenty republics in comparison with the United States offsets their legal equality. Although small states may wish to escape from great power domination by secession and a nonalignment policy, they may be impelled to retain their alliance ties in order guarantee a continual flow of economic and military aid from the great power.

The type of political and military disparity present within most regional structures, however, is more the result rather than the cause of differences in the power of nation-states. One of the most outstanding characteristics of the contemporary state system has been the progressive decline in the number of major powers over the past century which may be attributed more to the debilitating effects of war and depression than to the tendency for regional blocs to assume defense functions formerly entrusted to individual states. Changes in the world balance of power that produced bipolarity in 1945 are intimately related to the gradual decline of the power of the major European states as a result of the devastation of World War I and World War II, the breakup of colonial empires through anti-imperialist revolutions, and the startling increase in the national power of the United States and the Soviet Union. As a consequence, the balance of power system changed from a complex and flexible structure of several equally powerful units into a simple and rigid con-

frontation of two major powers exacerbated by diametrically opposed
ideologies. The formation of mutually antagonistic regional systems
so prominent since 1945 is therefore less the cause of international
instability as it is the reflection of changes in the structure of world
power and ideology that displaced the earlier patterns of the international state system.

The Theory of Multiple Equilibrium. Related to the previous discussion of the influence of the balance of power on contemporary
international organization is a theory of regionalism developed by
Professor George Liska who has perceptively analyzed the internal
and external aspects of regionalism, including the problem of maintaining a balance between universalism and regionalism.

Drawing upon the theory of economic equilibrium of micro-eco-
nomics, Liska applies the concept of equilibrium to the "international
organization of security and international relations in general." [19] As
a norm and as an actual state of affairs in the operation of political
institutions, the concept of a multiple institutional equilibrium is
introduced with respect to the structure, commitment of member units,
and geographic and functional scope of general and regional organizations. [20]

According to the theory, an international organization is in structural
equilibrium "if there is an over-all correspondence between the
margins of restraints it imposes on members and their willingness
to tolerate them and if the relations between the influence exercised
by individual members and their actual power are not too unequal. . . . " [21] Compatibility between obligations assumed and the
willingness to fulfill them ensures balance while functional equilibrium
is attained where functions are related to needs; geographic scope is
in equilibrium where the geographic area of the functional obligations
is adequate for their performance. [22]

The theory is said to be a function of multiple forces that tend to
influence the equilibrium or disequilibrium of international organizations through "a dynamic interplay of institutional, military-
political, and socio-economic factors and pressures." [23] Professor Liska
concludes the introduction of his basic hypotheses by asserting
"that a workable organization on national, regional, or global scale
requires that institutional, military-political, and socio-economic factors and pressures for and against stability be deliberately equilibrated." [23]

Although the theory of multiple equilibrium has important implications for the study of the relationship between regionalism and
universalism, it is essentially a restatement in different terms of
classical balance of power principles rather than a new formulation.
The key variables of institutional and socio-economic factors are
essentially derivatives of the military-political balance of power rather
than independent of it as suggested in the theory. Within the state
system institutional and socio-economic forces are conditioned more
by the operation of the military-political balance of power than
determinative of it. This may be illustrated in two ways.

The weakness of the United Nations as an institutional actor and
the disequilibrium consequent with the proliferation of regional
security systems reflects the rigidity inherent in a bipolar balance
of power. The two superpowers seek political strength in regional
systems whose membership shares the same ideological motivations
rather than in dependence upon a universal actor whose response to
their security needs may be halting and ineffective. International
institutional structures are thereby a function of the actual distribution
of world power rather than shapers of the distribution. This does not
imply that regional and universal institutions have no influence upon
the great powers but only that such influence is apt to be minimal in
deflecting them from their major political and ideological goals.

Similarly, the prevailing socio-economic forces operating within the
institutional system may also be viewed in terms of the distribution
of national power outside of it. The contemporary imbalance in socio-
economic levels favoring the industrialized nations seriously affects
the United Nations in that it is a continuing source of envy among
the less developed states within the organization. Such socio-economic
disparities are a product of an imbalance in military-political power
that had existed for centuries under Western colonialism and before
the rise of international organizations. They no doubt complicate the
internal environment of international institutions such as the United
Nations and affect the policy of that organization which is increasingly dominated by the smaller powers. Outside of the United
Nations, however, the smaller nations are subordinate to the distribution of military-political power of the United States and the Soviet
Union.

Despite the above critique, the theory of multiple equilibrium is
useful if it is understood that the dynamics of the balance of power

are fundamental and that institutional and socio-economic forces affecting international organization are derivatives of it.

In his discussion of universalism and regionalism Professor Liska argues that the advantage of regional cooperation and its compatibility with universalism "depend on the extent to which the two forms are in reciprocal equilibrium." [25] The problem of maintaining a balance between universalism and regionalism is perhaps the most difficult problem of modern international organization; yet the methods for solving or managing it have received only general consideration by scholars. Applying equilibrium theory, Professor Liska specifies the prerequisites for global-regional equilibrium: a correspondence between the functions of universal and regional organizations and their geographic area, membership, and needs, and mutual reinforcement of the two forms through differentiation of functions and mutual integration under the over-all control of the more inclusive body. [26] These may only be promoted through a differentiation and integration which limits regional organizations to regional problems, relegatng priority to inter-regional and universal concerns to the world organization by means of a subordination of regional agencies. [27]

As all of these prerequisites have been lacking in contemporary international organization, it is no wonder that a profound disequilibrium between universalism and regionalism has developed. A question that is not considered by Liska but which seems pertinent is whether the mutual integration of regionalism and universalism presupposes the existence of an underlying world solidarity. It is the opinion of the author that the type of centralized control of regional agencies necessary for reciprocal equilibrium would be possible only and until the state system is drastically transformed into a genuine world community in which loyalties were redirected beyond the nation-state to the world organization. Given the contemporary entrenchment of state sovereignty and nationalism, it is questionable whether the integration of regionalism and universalism is feasible in the forseeable future except by a forcible predominance of one power or group of powers.

Toward a Definition of Regionalism. In order to ascertain the nature of regionalism as a phenomenon of international relations, it is necessary to define what constitutes a region. Unfortunately, there is a lack of agreement on a definition with the result that the term region has been justified as a geographical area, a cultural entity, an economic unit, a political division or a combination of all of these elements. As Professor Claude has observed, "rational regional divisions are difficult to establish, boundaries determined for one purpose are not necessarily appropriate for other purposes." [28]

There are many examples available to demonstrate the ambiguities of the term region. The North Atlantic is considered a region for military security for NATO, but that agency includes Greece and Turkey, nations geographically removed from the Atlantic Ocean. Western Europe may be viewed as a natural economic region, but it has been arbitrarily bifurcated into the competitive subregional systems of the European Free Trade Association (EFTA) and the European Economic Community (EDC) because political disagreements have overshadowed economic affinities. Geographic propinquity is not necessarily a precondition for regionalism as revealed in the geographical separation of the Asian members of the Southeast Asia Treaty Organization (SEATO) and especially by the participation of non-regional states in that organization.

For Professor Padelford, however, geography is an essential element of regionalism since regions are ". . . spatial areas which come to be spoken of as 'regions' as a result of usage stemming from the practices of groups of states, utterance of statesmen, or the terms of treaties or agreements between groups of states." [29] But region is also defined as ". . . limited to sovereign states within a certain area or having common interests in that area." [30] This would seem to apply to SEATO where the non-Asian members have a common interest in preventing the spread of communism in a region with which they are not geographically contiguous.

As used in this study the term region will denote a geographic area comprised of a number of independent states sharing common economic, social, and political values and goals. If this is accepted as a working definition subject to the qualifications cited above, a number of difficulties still remain. Are any international problems so exclusively regional that they may be objectively determined? Presumably if this were possible a more rational division of labor between universal and regional organizations might be possible.

Closer examination, however, discloses that the subject matter of international relations cannot be neatly categorized. Certain problems transcend geographic regions and demand universal action in order to be solved though regional agencies may supplement the universal organization. For example economic underdevelopment exists among several regions, and, while regional cooperation may be appropriate, the nations in such regions are too impoverished to provide the funds necessary for national and regional needs and solicit the United Nations and extra-regional states for support. Similarly, the reduction or elimination of the arms race through control of armaments cannot be localized since nuclear weapons technology is rapidly spreading to a number of regions. As nations become more interdependent through improvements in transportation and communications, the line of demarcation between regional and universal problems becomes increasingly blurred if not indistinguishable. This makes it all the more difficult to stipulate in advance the proper spheres of action for universal and regional organizations and increases the need for simultaneous cooperation.

In the continual debate between universalists and regionalists, Professor I. L. Claude finds that "the regionalist position is that the regional unit is capable of more effective organizational action than the global unit; the stress is placed here on the nature of the unit rather than the nature of the problem." [31] If this view is correct, and much of the advocacy of regionalism stresses the greater homogeneity of nations at the regional level, equilibrium between regionalism and universalism in practice would seem to defy a deliberate and rational differentiation of functions and depend primarily on political expediency.

The tendency to separate needs from capacity for action has created "one of the basic dilemmas of international organization: the disparity between needs for organization and capacity for organization." [32] To the extent that this disparity is wide, we may perceive a disequilibrium between regionalism and universalism. Whether the dilemma implies a choice between treating issues on the basis of their inherent nature or on the basis of the most effective organizational response is not clear. [33] It is quite possible that simultaneous action may obviate the necessity of a dichotomy between the two approaches.

Pitman B. Potter has argued that "the principal task . . . is not to waste time debating over regionalism versus universalism, but to study the ways in which in concrete cases the two principles can be utilized in combination and the standards to be applied in determining the dosage of each to be adopted." [34]

Disequilibrium might be checked and duplication and conflict avoided if regional agencies could be made genuinely subordinate to the universal organization. This would involve "a workable compromise between the requisite autonomy for regional arrangements and their equally necessary subordination to central authority" in order to prevent regional groupings from degenerating into competitive power blocs because of a weakened central organization. [35]

It is well known that this compromise has not been forthcoming since 1945 and does not appear likely in the immediate future. As a result the following characteristics of global-regional disequilibrium or imbalance may be noted: (1) the global organization superseded as the principal enforcement agency for collective security; (2) advanced military integration and planning transferred to regional alliances; (3) the world organization reduced from an enforcement to a conciliatory mechanism; and (4) ensuing competition among regional alliances. [36]

Events since 1945 confirm these characteristics. The United Nations no longer functions as the central agency for the enforcement of peace and security. Its functions have been appropriated by a myriad of regional agencies ranging from the NATO system to the Warsaw Pact both of which have attained a high degree of military-strategic integration and planning. With the role of the United Nations limited to conciliation and debate, major prominence has shifted to the various regional security agencies of the United States and the Soviet Union. Interlocked in continuing competition that involves not only dangerous direct confrontation as in Berlin but also an unremitting struggle for the allegiance of the expanding number of uncommitted countries, the unregulated rivalry of competing regional bloc systems intensifies international conflict and threatens the possible extinction of the modern state system. But this is a matter to be discussed toward the conclusion of this study.

Characteristic of Regional Solidarity. Thus far we have been chiefly concerned with the external aspects of regionalism. Although regional cooperation is affected by the strength or weakness of the universal organization and by inter-regional relationships, regional politics also determines the solidarity of member states. Inquiry into the nature of intra-regional politics requires an analysis of two basic questions: (1) what are the elements which make up a stable regional system and (2) what conclusions may be drawn with regard to the efficacy of small-state regionalism and regional associations clustered around one or more great powers?

Earlier some characteristics were presented that account for the cooperation that is theoretically possible among states within a specific region. In addition to geographic proximity, the existence of a similar political, ideological, social, and cultural background were cited as unifying elements.

Perhaps the most comprehensive attempt to analyze the elements that comprise a "stable" regional system is the study by B. Bhoutros-Ghali. [37] Approaching the study as a political sociologist, he draws on the insights of both disciplines to enlighten our understanding of the substructure of regional associations. While the principles presented are normative in character and somewhat idealistic, they constitute a major contribution to an appreciation of the interrelated aspects of regional solidarity.

Regional groups are said to be composed of a mixture of necessary and sufficient elements. The following necessary elements include: (legal) a treaty for the maintenance of peace; (sociological) a treaty based on a particular sociological solidarity embracing racial or ethnic affinities, economic cooperation, mutual defense; (geographic) contiguity of member states and (institutional) an international agency of a permanent character.

In addition to these necessary elements, regional groups require for their success the following: legal equality of member states; free adhesion; and more than five signatories.

Necessary and sufficient elements are interdependent and mutually reinforcing since regional systems that depend upon a single element of solidarity "will be condemned to failure to the extent [that] they are not based on different elements which are interconnected." [38] While this is an assumption that has not yet been verified by empirical research, there is increasing acceptance of its validity among scholars. The persistent internal conflicts within NATO, for example, have frequently been attributable to a juridical structure too narrowly based on military solidarity.

According to Bhoutros-Ghali, the various elements of sociological solidarity constitute the substructure upon which are superimposed provisions for pacific settlement, use of force, juridical structure, and economic and social cooperation. Regional solidarity is further defined in terms of three aspects: a series of primary elements existing prior to any human will such as the belief in a bond of imaginary race, belonging to a similar complex history, the existence of a given geographical situation, and certain consciousness of group sentiment that dominates in time of crisis. [39]

In the discussion of geographical contiguity as a prerequisite for regional cooperation, a distinction is made between direct contiguity and interposition in which a number of states have a common interest in a region but are themselves not contiguous with each other. [40] For example, Argentina and the United States are not geographically contiguous but both have a common interest in the Western Hemisphere which is realized by their membership in the Organization of American States. The earlier cited example of the association of geographically separated states in the SEATO is also illustrative of interposition.

If some degree of geographic contiguity is a basic element of a regional system, the region itself is not susceptible to geographic precision. Ultimately, regions are defined politically according to the power capabilities of states, for while natural barriers may separate one region from another they have not prevented states from establishing spheres of influence far removed from the home territory.

Political relations among the members of regional groups often pose difficult problems of dependency as suggested earlier. [41] One view is that "the only basis upon which regional arrangements can be made to function . . . is that of mutual respect for the sovereignty and independence of all members . . ." [42]

Although legal equality is mentioned by Bhoutros-Ghali as necessary to perfect a regional system, he does recognize the disparity between legal equality and political inequality in those systems dominated by one or more great powers. These elements are relatively balanced only in those small state regional systems which, unfortunately, have not demonstrated much durability or strength.

Whether the discrepancy between political inequality and legal equality that is characteristic of Western regional systems will bring about their dissolution is debatable. Coalitions under the domination of a great power, according to Bhoutros-Ghali, "will [lead to] . . . a restricted union provoking the dislocation of the general union; soon the general union will disengage itself; each small state taking refuge in its former independence." [43] Although disintegrative tendecies are visible in the Western coalition systems of NATO, OAS, and SEATO, they have not been powerful enough to bring about their termination. If the threat of Soviet and Chinese aggression were to recede, it is nuclear whether NATO and SEATO would sur-

vive. The answer would seem to depend on whether other bonds
of cooperation could be developed in which the member states could
channel their energies.

On the basis of the preceding description of the elements comprising a successful regional system, Professor Bhoutros-Ghali defines regional understandings (ententes) "as organisms of a permanent
character, grouping in a geographically determined region of more
than two states which by reason of their proximity, their communities of interests or their affinities, . . . [establish] an association for
the maintenance of peace and security in their region and for the
development of their economic, social and cultural cooperation with
the final purpose of forming a distinct political entity." [44]

The advantage of such a theoretical formulation of the ingredients
of regional solidarity is that it focuses on the anatomy if not the
institutional structure of regional systems. By probing the foundations that serve to unite nation-states, we are in a better position
to understand what is often vaguely referred to as the greater
homogeneity of regionalism in contrast to the world at large. However, there is a danger in overstressing similarities and understressing
differences and antagonisms that exist within regional groupings.
Geographically proximate states may not be friends but enemies as
in the classic case of France and Germany. Moreover, despite the
presence of a certain sociological solidarity or unity, Western Europe
was fragmented into competitive and autonomous units until quite
recently. In the Middle East a common Arab heritage has not proved
to be a sufficiently adequate basis for regional cohesion for a loosely
formed Arab League organization. Thus, despite social and cultural
similarities, nations and regions may be susceptible to disassociative
forces engendered by mutually competitive foreign policies that may
nullify all of the preexisting necessary and sufficient elements for
successful regionalism.

Secondly, while the sociological approach to regional solidarity is
useful, it neglects to explore the interaction between those elements
that predispose states to seek cooperation and the institutions created to fulfill such cooperation. Too little attention is devoted to
the importance of the institutional factor in retarding or accelerating
regional integration. Fortunately, this gap has been partially filled
by Professor Ernst Haas, who has developed two suggestive hypotheses regarding the influence of regional institutions on economic
and political integration in Western Europe: [45]

(1) A central institution will affect political integration meaningfully only if it is willing to follow policies giving rise to expectations
and demands for more—or fewer federal measures. If it fails to arouse
strong positive or negative responses, its impact is apt to be minimal.

(2) Regional integration involves a complex interaction among
international institutions, national governments, national and supranational parties, and national and supranational pressure groups in
which "major interest groups as well as politicians determine their
support of, or opposition to, new central institutions and policies on
the basis of a calculation of advantage."

Haas believes these conclusions are valid not only for Western
Europe but for other areas in which there is a similarly high level of
industrialism, parliamentary or presidential democracy, identifiable
elites, and articulate and literate masses mobilized for political action.

Though Bhoutros-Ghali acknowledges the significance of economic
factors for regional cooperation, he seems to view regional economic
cooperation as less desirable than universal economic cooperation.
Yet if the latter ideal is unattainable states may be disposed to
initiate regionalism in the economic sphere. The desire for economic
advantage has proven to be a powerful stimulus to the creation of
regional unity in Western Europe since 1945. With less economic
justification, the European experience is being imitated in many non-
European areas. This is not to imply that the basis of regionalism is
primarily economic or to deny that regional economic unity may
indeed be discriminatory toward non-regional states, but only to
indicate that regional economic cooperation has been of such importance that it is necessary to emphasize that of all of the elements
undergirding regional solidarity the expectation of economic advantage is increasingly significant.

Should the object of regional groups include the eventual formation of a political union? In reply to the question of whether it is
not harmful to indicate in advance to states that the final purpose
of their association is to lose their independence, Bhoutros-Ghali
asserts that a study of the various elements of a regional understanding reveals: [46] "that there . . . is a natural tendency [for regional
groups] to tighten their ties. History teaches us . . . that this tendency has been helpful several times in making evolution of several
of these communities from an anarchial or weakly organized state
to a federal state. [It is an evolutionary goal which] does not neces-

sitate a formal acceptance by members; nevertheless, the latter are presumed to recognize this purpose as one of the elements of regional life and should adapt themselves to it."

Examination of these assumptions, however, may result in somewhat different conclusions. The experience of the American colonies and the Swiss cantons does reveal tendencies that culminated in an amalgamation of previously separate units as discussed in a recent study on the formation of political community.[47] But this does not necessarily warrant analogy with contemporary regional agencies. The two cases involved the expansion of community within essentially national settings not the integration of a number of states into a regional community. Also, the period involved the 18th and early 19th centuries before the rise of industrialization and mass political movements. However, it is conceivable that future studies may demonstrate that those factors which precipitate the unification of national states also operate internationally.

Conversely, certain factors may affect international integration that do not affect national integration. What are such factors? It is still premature to be scientific, but intuitive examination of the process of European integration since 1945 suggests that a certain disillusionment with traditional nationalism coupled with an appreciation of the economic and political advantages of regional unification were instrumental in launching regional unity. Until more is known about the differences and similarities between national and international integration, however, it should not be assumed that there is an inevitable evolution of regional groups toward centralized or federalized structures. There are too many variables that may impede a process of regional integration well under way. The French veto of Great Britain's admission into the European Common Market in January, 1963, provides a recent illustration. Regional groups may have the potential to expand into supranational political communities, but they may also be vulnerable to disintegrative forces.

Small State Regionalism and the Theory of Great Power Orbits. An inquiry into the internal dynamics of regionalism would be incomplete if it were limited only to an appreciation of the factors predisposing independent states to merge in cooperation. A vital aspect of all regional groups involves not only the strength of the interests which bind but an understanding of the relative political influences of the member states. These influences may be integrative (centripetal) or distintegrative (centrifugal); they may involve large and small states.

The case for small state regionalism has been stated in terms of an antipathy toward great power domination and with a frank contempt for their qualities: [49]

"International regionalism favors in the spiritual interest of the world, the survival of small and middle powers, in the midst of which a qualitative civilization can develop through opposition to the quantitative civilization proper for the great modern powers, and if the regional arrangements complete only that mission, that would be sufficient to justify their existence. . . ."

In his analysis of the dynamics of small state regional organizations, however, Professor Liska expresses grave doubts about their viability as summarized below: [50]

(1) Small state regionalism is impractical because of the inadequacy of weak powers to ensure regional security and welfare.

(2) While small states value participation in a world organization, they are attracted to regional groups where their national security may be guarantted by great powers.

(3) Study of the Arab League and the Little Entente reveals a number of inherent disadvantages of small state regional cooperation.

Specifically, study of the Little Entente and the Arab League reveals some of the limitations of small-state groups:

• Both brought together minor states formerly belonging to large empires situated in strategic areas but with inadequate defensive power.

• The incentive to association in both instances was negative— the Arab states to offset Israel the Little Entente to check Hungary and Bulgaria.

•While both groups desired to expel great power influence (France from the Middle East and Russia, Italy, and Germany from Balkans) they needed the aid of outside powers for stability: France to support the Little Entente and the United States and Britain to aid the Arab League.

Liska concluded that the lack of a centralized structure, an exacting security commitment to repel aggression, and the absence of positive goals militated against the achievement of a closer unity despite a common cultural and historical tradition. The fact that both systems could not isolate their policies from the wider world distribution of power, especially the activities and pressures of the major powers, was another cause of their failure.

Do these conclusions, drawn from an examination of only two small-state regional groups, constitute sufficient evidence to condemn such associations as ineffective? The answer would appear to be affirmative if such agencies are assessed in terms of their record of deterring aggression since the Little Entente and the Balkan Entente failed to preserve regional security. On the other hand, while these groups achieved only token economic and social cooperation, the possibility of such cooperation among small states cannot be excluded. In fact, the emergence of customs union arrangements recently in Latin America, Africa, and the Middle East is based on the feasibility of partnership among smaller nation for economic and social development, including eventual elimination of abnormal economic dependence on the wealthier states. The difficulties should not be minimized in view of the fervent nationalism that envelops these areas and the considerable economic and social improvements necessary. It is premature to evaluate the success of such efforts, but it is possible that they may be useful especially if the participating nations recognize that national integration is an important precondition for effective regional cooperation. [51]

More difficult and more controversial than small state regionalism is whether "a more promising alternative might be regional groupings anchored in the superior resources of a nuclear Great Power." [50] As this has been the most common type of regional arrangement, a thorough examination of the merits and defects of such groupings is required.

The intrusion or participation of one or more great powers in a regional complex is the strongest factor in altering its narrow geographic scope since the interests of such states are increasingly global. As a result the regional body tends to ". . . lose its geographic sense as well as its assured emancipation from involvement in the unwelcome complexities of the wide world." [53] An interesting example may be found in the recent history of the inter-American system of which the Organization of American States is the political and juridical expression. In spite of the increase in hemispheric solidarity expressed in the Rio Pact and the consolidation and extension of informal pre-war cooperation through the OAS, that agency was hampered in its formative period because the United States as the dominant great power relegated Latin America to a relatively low priority in its foreign policy and concentrated on Western Europe and the Far East where it was involved in balance of power politics against the Soviet Union.

The aftermath of this policy of polite neglect produced intra-regional resentment and criticism of the United States for its abandonment of earlier stated proposals to strengthen inter-American solidarity. Between 1948 and 1960 Latin America provided a classic illustration of a region in which a great power's global responsibilities undermined the cohesion of a regional system with which it had long been identified as the leading state. The Castro-led Cuban revolution of 1959 and the ensuing instability it created within Latin America may have served as a healthy antidote to the period of relative neglect by redirecting the attention of the United States to the difficult problem of containing the spread of communism to other parts of the hemisphere. Whether its heightened interest in the region as expressed by the Alliance for Progress program will be able to revitalize the inter-American system is not clear. In any event the motivation for increased great power concern was not precipitated by humanitarian consideration for the welfare of Latin America, but was inextricably linked with the world wide ideological struggle between communism and democracy.

A much more common criticism of regional systems geared to great powers is that the increment in national security gained by the participation of small states in such systems is often more than offset by the gradual erosion of their independence.* Another common indictment of regionalism is that rival regional groups degenerate into competing "spheres of influence" that lead to international instability rather than to international equilibrium.

To see the problem in clearer perspective, it is necessary to study the theory and practice of great power orbits. Theories contemplating a world order of regional superpowers were developed during World War II by Walter Lippmann and E. H. Carr and need to be studied separately from their pragmatic application brought about by the disintegration of the World War II alliance system.[54]

The theory of great power orbits is based on the premise that "re-

---

*The obvious illustration is the Soviet dominated Warsaw Pact, but it may also be visible in lesser degree within the inter-American and North Atlantic defense systems. It is a moot point, however, as to whether the Warsaw system represents a genuine regional association inasmuch as the legal independence and sovereignty of the East European satellites is more fictional than real.

gional groupings of small states ought to cluster around the local
Great Power and pool military, economic, and other resources in
peace and war." [55] The arrangement would help the great power by
supplying it with additional facilities and give to the smaller powers
aid, protection, and a degree of independence thereby enhancing intra-
regional and inter-regional security. [56]

Regional orbits managed by great powers may be justified on the
basis of three additional assumptions: the ability of great powers to
insure regional security; the compatibility of interests between the
regional great power and small states; and the disposition of great
powers to develop policies of restraint toward their lesser allies.
Empirical analysis, however, casts doubt on the validity of each of
these premises. In an era of nuclear stalemate, great powers are unable
to guarantee the security of their satellites against surprise attack;
there is often conflict between the great power and its associates who
tend to resent their power inferiority; and the necessity of maintaining
regional solidarity may dispose the great power to exert periodic
pressure or even coercion on recalcitrant smaller powers.

An elaboration of the theory of great powers postulates the coexistence of a number of regional systems controlled by great powers
that would undergird and strengthen world order. Winston Churchill,
for example, believed that a universal order based on the general
concept of collective security had proved to be too ambitious during
the inter-war period and needed to be replaced by regionalized security
systems. Early in World War II he supported the idea of a regionalized world organization: [57]

"It is the intention of the Chiefs of the United Nations to create
a world organization for the preservation of peace, based upon conceptions of freedom and justice and the revival of prosperity. As a
part of this organization an instrument of European government
will be established which will embody the spirit but not be subject
to the weakness of the former League of Nations. The units forming
this body will not only be the great nations of Europe and Asia Minor
as long established, but a number of Confederations formed among
the smaller states, among which a Scandinavian Bloc, a Danubian
Bloc, and a Balkan Bloc appear to be obvious. A similar instrument
will be formed in the Far East, with different membership. . . ."

Thus under the theory "a general international organization is
reduced to a secondary role or renounced altogether." [59]

Insofar as the politics of great power orbits are concerned, the tendency is for fluctuation between domination of the smaller power and a reconciliation of "the legitimate regional interests (of the great power) with the rights of the smaller nations." [60] But in the absence of external countervailing pressures, it is difficult for even a liberally oriented major power to avoid periodic interference.

Within the British Empire and the Western Hemisphere a pattern of intra-regional power originally based upon satellitism has progressively evolved to near parnership primarily because of the liberal values and ideologies of the dominant powers—the United States and Great Britain. [61] Yet the problem of developing coequal partnership rather than domination has been difficult. The inter-American system has been weakened not only because of extra-regional problems demanding the attention of the United States; the enormous disparity between the economic and political power of the United States and the other Latin American nations precludes the emergence of political equality which the concept of partnership presupposes.

While the establishment of the Commonwealth of Nations was a pragmatic attempt by an imperial power to perpetuate its influence among former dependencies and thereby offset "the end of empire," this unique association has also experienced disintegrative forces that jeopardize its cohesion. The decline of Great Britain as a major power undermined the protective foundation upon which the solidarity of the "old" Commonwealth was based, causing Canada, Australia, and New Zealand to seek new security ties with the United States. Expansion of the membership to include non-white and non-western states in Africa and the Far East further eroded the family-like atmosphere that prevailed among the older and more homogenous Commonwealth members. But the potentially most divisive factor confronting the Commonwealth is the possible entry of Britain into the European Common Market and with it the abandonment of the traditional British policy of aloofness from continental European politics. Though it may be possible for Britain to work out some pattern of compromise of her emerging loyalties to Europe with her traditional ties to the Commonwealth, it is unlikely that the latter will ever be as viable an association as in the past.

As a result of the imperfections of the great power orbits described above, the smaller nations within the inter-American system and the Commonwealth have sought a counterweight to their dependency by active participation in the United Nations. The Latin American nations especially have displayed a curious fluctuation between re-

gionalism and universalism. Dependent upon the United States for
military and economic security, they are fearful of the effect of such
dependency upon their independence and paradoxically disgruntled
whenever the United States becomes preoccupied with the problems
of other regions. They seek solace for their insecurity in the United
Nations which they value as "a forum for their own extra-hemispheric
self-affirmation" and utilize as "an additional potential check on the
Colossus of the North." [62]

With regard to the Commonwealth and the inter-American system,
it is possible that the major powers and their lesser allies may find
participation in the universal and regional organizations mutually
beneficial depending upon the circumstances of the moment. As
will be analyzed in a later chapter, the flight to regional security
agencies after 1945 developed as a result of uncertainty regarding
the efficacy of the collective security mechanism of the United
Nations. Although membership in the general organization for the
United States and its Western European allies still proves useful
and indeed necessary, there is a greater security advantage within
the more limited association of NATO whose collective security obligations are automatic rather than conditional. Similarly, regional
agencies may prove advantageous as dispute-settling mechanisms
as in the success of the Organization of American States in quelling
minor regional disputes before they could be exploited by the Soviet
Union.

Contrarily, outright incompatibility between regionalism and universalism is symbolized by the policies of the Soviet Union. It
considers participation in the global organization a tactical necessity
while working constantly to weaken the United Nations as a peace-
keeping agency. Efforts to strengthen the solidarity of the Warsaw
Pact organization have been given greater emphasis in recent years.

Plausible though the theory of great power orbits may be, it is
fraught with numerous defects when applied in practice. The basic
difficulty is the tendency of great powers to manipulate and control
their lesser allies unless ideology serves as a restraint against interventionism. The theory assumes self-restraint but does not provide
any defense for small nations in the event that the great power displays
expansionist proclivities. Possible defenses include the utilization of
the general organization to focus world opinion on great power
machinations, solicitation of assistance from an extra-regional great
power, or ultimately secession from the regional system. Resort to

one or more of these techniques would not only be indicative of the lack of compatibility between the great power and its smaller allies but also potentially dangerous to the solidarity of the regional system.

These observations may serve to heighten our awareness of the difficulty of regional isolation in the contemporary international system. In a system in which there is likely to be a continuous and changing interaction among three types of actors—powerful extra-regional states, the United Nations, and the regional system itself—the difficulties of sustaining regional groupings apart from the wider system appear obvious.

Does this necessarily lead to the conclusion that the theory "stands for the enlargement of the vertical power of the nuclear state typical of imperialism?"[64] Although this tendency was discernible in the early phase of the NATO system because the European nations were peculiarly dependent on the United States for military and economic assistance, it has been reversed by the gradual economic and political unification of Western Europe and the possible possession of nuclear weapons by small states within the alliance.

Within the other regional agencies headed by the United States, a comparable reduction of power disparity has not developed, but this does not necessarily mean that the gap in power that now exists is destined to continue. As the weaker members of these coalitions make a successful transition to economic and political modernization, they may be able to reduce their overwhelming contemporary dependence upon the great power.

A second limitation of the theory pertains to the alleged cohesion which a great power may stimulate within regional groupings by virtue of its superior economic and military resources. Yet it is doubtful that the interests of such powers can be centered exclusively within one region. This may lead to a neglect of the smaller powers as reflected in the American policy toward Latin America before 1960. Also, because of the tendency of security zones to overlap, increasing pressures may be generated on the great power to solidify control over its allies in an effort to compete with rival regional systems for the allegiance of intermediate smaller states.[65] The uncommitted states that interpose themselves between the Western and Soviet blocs are an obvious example of the overlapping of security zones.

As mentioned earlier, insofar as there is a tendency of great powers toward imperialism, it may be counteracted by a restraining ideology, the external pressures of the general organization, or by the intrusion of a rival great power. Using the NATO and OAS systems as models, we may perceive that the intra-regional dynamics of these great power orbits appear to be governed by fluctuations ranging from expansionism of the great power toward a more progressive sharing of responsibilities with the smaller powers.

Finally, the theory of great power orbits is open to criticism if viewed as a panacea for international stability. It assumes that an inter-regional equilibrium is facilitated by regionally dominated great-power systems. But this is hardly possible unless regional blocs are headed by powers of a similar ideology. Moreover, even if such a constellation of ideologically compatible blocs could be developed, there would still be the possibility of inter-regional conflict arising out of the extra-regional interests of major powers unless the regional blocs were equilibrated and reconciled within the framework of a universal international organization. In turn this would require the relinquishment of great power regional hegemony for equilibrium between the global organization and a series of regional blocs through the subordination of the latter to the former. How could such an arrangement be managed if the organization of peace and security was centralized among a number of regional blocs and decentralized at the universal level?

A more effective approach to world order than a series of unregulated regional blocs is one in which regional systems are subordinated and controlled by the universal organization. Such an approach, however, would require the revitalization of the United Nations as a peace enforcement agency. As long as the major powers entrust their security to regional bloc systems rather than to the United Nations, that organization will be impotent as a collective security mechanism and the global-regional equilibrium posited by the United Nations Charter inoperative.

Furthermore, the contemporary trend toward regional integration may slow down universal integration if the consolidation of regions and their coexistence within the general organization accentuates their identities and interests. [66] The universal system will then remain what it is now: an arena for minimizing conflict and maximizing common interests in deference to a minimum common denominator. [67]

A more optimistic view of the contemporary situation, however, is presented by Professor Inis Claude: [68]

"It should be emphasized that the United Nations is irrelevant to the security issue posed by great-power conflict only in a very partial and limited sense. The Organization is incapable of exercising coercive control over a great power. It cannot prevent or suppress aggression by major powers; it cannot prevent war among them; hence, it cannot promise protection to any state against the ravages of war launched by a great power. However, the rules of the Charter prohibiting the aggressive use of force are assuredly applicable to the rival great powers, despite the fact that their enforcement cannot under present conditions be institutionalized; the Charter excused the United Nations from the effort to enforce these rules against the great powers, but it does not excuse the latter from the obligation to respect them. Moreover, the United Nations is relevant in the sense that it possesses a variety of resources which may be used . . . to influence the behavior of the major powers toward each other and toward lesser states, to promote the moderation of conflict. . . . The regional groupings are the organizations of force relevant to the crisis in great-power relationships. The relevance of the United Nations is of a different, but not necessarily inferior, order."

It is by no means certain, however, whether the United Nations would be able to play such a definitive role in the case of direct confrontation of the superpowers as in Berlin. As Professor Claude himself admits, the United Nations has been effective mainly in those conflicts where the confrontation is indirect such as in the Suez Crisis of 1956 and in the Congo Crisis of 1960. [69] In such conflicts United Nations peace forces have functioned as agencies of interposition sealing off the area in dispute from the direct clash of the superpowers. But this is a much more modest role for the United Nations than was contemplated in the Charter inasmuch as these international forces have been utilized only after first obtaining the consent of the states involved in the dispute rather than exercising an independent coercive power.

A Theory of Isolation and Collaboration. To conclude this discussion of theories of regionalism, we will now examine a recent theoretical model constructed by Professor Harold Guetzkow that further explores the complex interrelationship between regionalism and universalism. [70] The distinctiveness of his contribution arises from the fact that it illuminates two variables that are crucial in the life of nations —isolation and collaboration—and attempts to predict future trends toward isolation or collaboration on the basis of the past experience of states. His conclusions may be applied to the behavior of regional groupings in two ways: (1) collaborationist tendencies of individual nations result in efforts toward the integration of a group of nations; and (2) as regional entities emerge they may exhibit tendencies of inward isolation or outward collaboration toward the universal organization.

The model postulates the opposition of isolation and collaboration factors said to influence the behavior of certain types of groups such as the labor union, city council, and the nation-state. Following are some of the factors that operate to direct the behavior of groups inward, other things being equal:

(1) Experience with self-reliance has been favorable to solve needs.

(2) Ideologies of the group are oriented toward isolation.

(3) Self-reliant means to achieve goals are more advantageous and practical than collaborative means.

(4) The tasks of the group permit it to pursue its goal or goals in isolation.

(5) Members feel collaboration interferes with successful self-reliance.

(6) The leadership of the group fears collaboration will undermine its position.

To the extent that these factors are reversed, the direction of behavior will turn outward into collaboration.

It is not necessary to reproduce the model in its entirety here but rather to extrapolate those features of it that clarify the theoretical aspects of the interaction between universal and regional organizations.

In determining the behavior of groups certain past experience factors are influential in predicting how new demands will be met. As might be expected, the greater the satisfaction of needs through internal or self-reliant measures, the greater the tendency for internal solutions as new needs arise; conversely, to the extent that such needs have been previously solved through inter-group relations, the more likely will collaboration with other groups be sought in the future.[n]

Some additional hypotheses of the model are:

(1) If new demands arise (to meet certain political or economic needs) or members believe that their existing demands are not being met satisfactorily, the following responses may occur: (a) members may try to satisfy their demands self-reliantly by making internal changes in the group itself, acting in isolation from other groups; and/or (b) members may try to satisfy their demands through cooperation with other groups by collaboration.

(2) If the needs of group members are relatively constant and relatively well satisfied, there will not be any significant impulse for change.

The direction of behavior of groups toward isolation or collaboration is determined by the following factors:

(1) The relative strengths of the factors of isolation and collaboration and their components "determine the direction of behavior."

(2) The direction of behavior may be thus complicated by equally strong pressures for isolation and collaboration thereby producing conflict within the group as to which direction to move. (Applied to regionalism, this hypothesis envisages a situation in which a regional organization may be pressured by forces tending toward exclusivism or toward cooperation with other regional agencies or the universal organization.)

(3) Stalemates will be produced when there is equilibrium of opposing factors of isolation and collaboration.

Do regional organizations hinder or support the development of universal agencies? On the basis of the preceding hypotheses, the model predicts "that the development of partially inclusive groups would tend to delay the growth of more inclusive universal organization, to the extent that partial arrangements are successful in meeting their members' goals." [72]

Is it possible, however, that this prediction neglects a crucial variable operative in the real world of international politics? Some needs will be satisfied only by simultaneous cooperation at both the regional and universal level rather than on the basis of mutually exclusive alternatives. For example, United States membership in the United Nations and in various regional agencies may be logically justified as consonant with the promotion of national security objectives at dual levels; small powers, too, may utilize a dual pattern to maximize their influence which may be weak in a regional agency dominated by a major power but stronger when acting as a member of a regional bloc in the General Assembly of the United Nations. On the other hand, many of the newly emerging nations have favored universalism over regionalism in their desire to maintain maximum maneuverability vis-a-vis the superpowers and thereby escape the domination which would ensue through participation in regional alliance systems.

Contemporary utilization of universalism may be the result of inadequate regional integration in the Western Hemisphere, Africa, Asia, and the Middle East. To the extent that regional agencies are not successfully satisfying the needs of individual states in these areas, they will seek assistance from the universal organization. Unable to supply the capital and technical experts necessary for economic development and industrialization, the underdeveloped nations turn to the United Nations and its specialized agencies for support as well as to individually prosperous nations outside of their regions.

If regional economic and political integration is realized in the underdeveloped regions, attention of national states would probably shift inwaard and away from the universal organization as Guetkow's model predicts. As such integration has only developed significantly within Western Europe, it is not surprising to find that the behavior of states within the non-Western regions is collaborative toward the universal organization. They frequently use the latter in order to compensate for their political and economic weakness through various bloc voting tactics designed to extract from the major powers the maximum commitments for economic development concerns; gradually, however, an incipient recognition of the utility of regional cooperation is emerging and may evolve into institutional arrangements of a multifunctional and transnational character.

In Western Europe, France, and to a lesser extent Belgium and Portugal, have adopted a semi-isolationist attitude toward the United Nations not only because burgeoning European economic and political unification is more satisfying to their needs but also because of the vehemence of criticism from the Afro-Asian bloc in the General Assembly for their colonial records. This may indicate that a corollary should be added to the model: the relationship between regionalism and universalism is conditioned not only by the degree of success with which regional communities satisfy the demands of their component member states but also by the nature of the experiences of individual nation-states in the universal organization.

One final example reinforces this observation. The threats of the Soviet bloc to leave the United Nations usually occur whenever its aims have been frustrated by United Nations action as for example in the defeat of their "troika" proposal to reorganize the administration of the Secretariat. Secession from the organization, however, would not be compensated by any tangible gain for the bloc. Nevertheless, the Soviet Union still cherishes as an ideal the goal of transforming the United Nations into a Communist controlled organization. [74] In the absence of the attainment of this goal, the universal organization may serve as a useful mechanism for Soviet propaganda but the bloc relies primarily on its own regional system, the Warsaw Pact, to serve its security needs.

Although there may be tendencies toward isolation from the universal organization as regional communities become integrated, it is unlikely that such tendencies will ever be absolute. The problems of regional systems cannot be totally isolated from the world community. In practice, it is impossible to exclude regional politics from world politics because of the pull of extra-regional interests affecting great power orbits. Similarly, while regional problems often require regional solutions, the impact of such problems upon other regions or the difficulty of solving them without some assistance from the universal organization militates against an automatic replacement of universalism as regional integration progresses. In matters involving disarmament, economic development, the control of outer space, and the expansion of international trade, a concerted effort by the entire international community is necessary. While the wider divergences of culture and economic and political policies at the world level may inhibit such cooperation, they do not make it any less vital or necessary.

Aside from the preceding observations, the various hypotheses advanced by Professor Guetzkow may invite certain objections. Can the nation-state or a regional system be classified as a group in common with entities of a more restricted character? If the theoretical model purports to explain the behavior of inter-group relations, does not the state possess certain attributes such as sovereignty that make it unique? In anticipation of such an objection, Professor Guetzkow declares that: [75] "The facts of international life indicated that states, like other groups, are circumscribed in their behavior by political, social, cultural and economic realities both within themselves and in their external environment. The leaders of nations, just like the leaders of other groups, are dependent for their very positions upon a complex structure of power within the group."

Acceptance of the assumption that the nation-state is a group exhibiting behavior characteristics not wholly dissimilar from other less inclusive and complex groups in regard to the variables of isolation/collaboration does not obscure the fact that there are basic differences among and within group structures. The interchangeability of nations, trade unions, city councils and political parties needs to be qualified by structural, socio-psychological, quantitative and qualitative distinctions. The nation-state operates in an environment

of greater complexity than sub-national groups because the former is
subject to the peculiar influences of the international environment
of states and regional and universal institutions in addition to the
customary domestic political and nonpolitical influences. Unlike the
state, the trade union, family, church, and city council function in a
more restricted and hence less complex milieu. Until we know more
about the variety of factors that impinge on the state as distinguished
from less inclusive groups, it would be premature to accept without
qualification the assumption that there is a basic similarity between
the isolation/collaboration behavior of the nation and other less
complex groups. The behavior of the nation is a composite of in-
finitely more variables than the behavior of even a major political
party or trade union which represents only a limited segment of the
nation. These qualifications seem to be recognized by Professor
Guetzkow in citing three limitations of his model: [76]

(1) The model does not enumerate all the factors which play an
important part in determining the direction of national/or sub-
group/behavior.

(2) The need to explore the socio-psychological mechanisms which
underlie isolation/collaboration behavior more adequately than developed in the model. For example, how do we measure or arrive at
or define the members' satisfaction that group is meeting their needs
and/or demands? How can we determine that there is dissatisfaction? Are these mechanisms more complex for the nation than for
the trade union?

(3) The model is only concerned with group policy; it does not
predict the form in which isolation/collaboration behavior will take.
For example, should problems be solved bilaterally or multilaterally
or both with regard to trade cooperation? Will collaborative behavior
be official or unofficial? The trend of behavior may be predicted by
the model but the important question of form is left vague.

Summary. The preceding survey of various theories of the regionalist approach to peace and security has attempted to delineate five
central aspects: the theoretical assumptions underlying regionalism
as a basis for international cooperation; the tangible and intangible
elements upon which regional systems are based; the internal political
dynamics of regional groupings involving the interaction of large and
small powers and its effect on regional cohesion; the difficult problem
of promoting global-regional equilibrium; and a theoretical considera-

tion of the factors that influence isolative and/or collaborative behavior of individual nations and regional alignments.

The purpose of this theoretical introduction has been to reveal both the advantages and limitations of the regional approach to peace and security, and especially to indicate the difficulty of divorcing regionalism from universalism in the real world of international politics. No attempt was made to suggest practical solutions for reconciling contemporary regionalism and universalism since the international system is so rigidified by ideological conflict as to preclude a reconciliation. In this connection, however, the author agrees with those scholars who believe that global-regional equilibrium can best be promoted by the subordination of regional agencies to the universal organization. Yet while in theory it may be possible to effect such a harmonization, in practice the contemporary disequilibrium does not appear susceptible to reversal in the foreseeable future.

The question of what is meant by the subordination of regional agencies of the United Nations does require some attention. It involves in the opinion of the author a return to the constitutional theory of the Charter of the United Nations which legitimized regional arrangements but provided for their control by the Security Council through Articles 52, 53, and 54. Yet the problem of effecting such a subordination is hardly constitutional but inherently political. In all likelihood the political prerequisite would be the emergence of a lasting consensus among the permanent members of the Council regarding the international status quo to be enforced. This would in turn imply an end to the ideological and power conflict between the United States and the Soviet Union that has gripped the world for nearly twenty years. Under such circumstances, regional agencies such as NATO and the Warsaw Pact organization would cease to operate as instrumentalities of conflict between the superpowers, and they and other security agencies could be more properly controlled in a revitalized United Nations system. Political equilibrium between universalism and regionalism would then be restored.

We turn now to a historical-analytical survey of regionalism based on an empirical examination of the development of regional agencies since the inception of the League of Nations in 1920. It is hoped that in the chapters to follow a clearer understanding of the strengths and weaknesses of the various theories of regionalism will be obtained.

CHAPTER III

REGIONALISM AND THE LEAGUE OF NATIONS

Although the striking growth of regional organizations is primarily a phenomenon of the period since World War II it is necessary to analyze the relations between universalism and regionalism that occurred during the inter-war period under the League of Nations. Regional groupings existed before 1920, but the absence of a permanent universal organization for peace and security precludes any meaningful analysis of the interrelationship of regionalism and universalism. During the inter-war period, a few regional security experiments were undertaken to supplement what were thought to be the inadequate security guarantees of the League of Nations Covenant. Prominent as regional systems were the Locarno Pacts, the Little Entente, and the Balkan Entente. In addition, the inter-American system formed before 1920 was not without significance.

The creation of regional agencies shortly after the establishment of the League of Nations reflects the cyclical charatcer of universalism and regionalism. In the decade between 1920-1930, the initial enthusiasm for the first great experiment in world organization was displaced by serious doubts as to whether the collective security commitment of the Covenant was an adequate enough safeguard for the deterrence of aggression. These doubts led to the formation of regional agencies designed to fill in the gaps in the Covenant and to function as adjuncts to the universal organization. Similarly, the non-implementation of the peace and security enforcement clauses of the United Nations Charter and the paralysis that afflicted the Security Council fostered a return to regionalism in the years immediately following World War II. In both instances regionalism arose as a pragmatic response to the inadequacies of universalism rather than as a deliberate attempt to inaugurate regional cooperation on the basis of an alleged theoretical superiority.

To understand the first phase in the operation of the cycle, we must examine the constitutional basis of the inter-relationship between regionalism and universalism as defined in the Covenant and the factors which precipitated the movement toward regional groupings in the years immediately following World War I.

It has been said that "the architects of the League did not aim deliberately at an equilibrium between the world organization and the regional understandings," and that "their respective functions were neither defined nor differentiated; joint membership of individual states in parallel systems would supply the main, if tenuous and often confusing link." [1] The explanation for this neglect lay in the attitude of the framers of the Covenant, who under the leadership of President Wilson, desired a strong universal organization that would not be weakened by explicit approval of regional agreements. It was widely held that such agreements in the form of alliances constituted a threat to the peace with the opposition of the Triple Alliance and the Triple Entente seen as a major cause of World War I.

Wilson's conception of a universal system of collective security in part reflected a conviction that neutrality was no longer feasible under conditions of modern warfare in view of the unsuccessful efforts of the United States to maintain its neutrality during 1914-1917. [2] He wished to replace balance of power arrangements with a new community of power: [3] "I am proposing that all nations henceforth avoid entangling alliances which would draw them into competition of power, catch them in a net of intrigue and selfish rivalry, and disturb their own affairs with influences intruded from without. There is no entangling alliance in a concert of power."

Clearly, this was a conception of security diametrically opposed to the old system of competing alliances and balance of power politics which had been a feature of the international system since its inception. On the basis of such sentiments Wilson in January, 1918, urged the formation of "a general association of nations . . . affording mutual guarantees of political independence and territorial integrity to great and small states alike."

In view of this universalist concept of peace and security, how can the concession to regionalism contained in Article 21 of the Covenant be explained? Wilson persuaded the other founders of the League to accept the article because he feared that the United States Senate would not approve the Covenant without it. [4] Article 21 provided that "Nothing in this Covenant shall be deemed to affect the validity of international engagements, such as treaties of arbitration or regional understandings like the Monroe doctrine, for securing the maintenance of peace."

But the Monroe Doctrine was in no sense a regional understanding. It was a unilateral declaration of policy by the United States without any standing under general international law. Insofar as the collective security provisions of the Covenant were concerned, recognition of the special status of the Doctrine did not imply that ". . . the Council or Assembly of the League were in any way debarred from applying the Covenant in the Western Hemisphere," but ". . . it was never possible to secure a clear admission of this fact from Washington." [5]

As a result of this ambiguity, the Latin American members of the League developed an ambivalent attitude toward the League of Nations. On the one hand they admitted the applicability of the Covenant to the Western Hemisphere but on the other they "considered it preferable, for reasons of pride, that American conflict should be settled without intervention from Europe or Asia." [6]

In a larger sense the absence of provisions in the Covenant for the coordination of universalism and regionalism may be traced to three factors: the general hostility of all members of the League (except France) to regional understandings and alliances; fear that control of regional systems would give them more importance than they merited; and the existence in the Covenant of certain provisions involving possible incompatibility between the League and regional understandings. [7]

Despite the lack of formal integration between the League and evolving regional systems, a type of informal coordination developed by virtue of the overlapping membership of various regional groupings and the League; representation was conceded to the members of the Little Entente on the League Council and while not implying express recognition of the regional understanding the practical result was the same. [8]

What were the factors responsible for the shift to regionalism that appeared shortly after the establishment of the League? Article 10 of the Covenant presupposed a community of nations obligated to guarantee the territorial integrity and independence of any state victimized by aggression through collective sanctions. But the mechanism for enforcing collective security appeared too vague to satisfy France and the smaller European powers of Central Europe especially after an interpretative resolution was introduced into the League Assembly in 1923 regarding Article 10. The resolution stipulated that [9] "It is for the constitutional authorities of each Member to decide in reference to the obligation of preserving the independence and integrity of the territory of Members, in what degree the Member is bound to assure the execution of this obligation by employment of its military forces."

Although the resolution was not adopted, it was considered as the authoritative interpretation of Article 10. Allowing each state to decide what assistance should be furnished in the event of aggression seriously weakened the character of military sanctions to be applied under Article 16 (2) of the Covenant. When combined with the failure of the United States to join the League, it prompted France to lead a return to the pre-war system of defensive alliances in order to maximize her security against a feared revival of German power.

Seizing on the loophole provided by Article 21, M. Bourgeois declared: "The whole idea of obligation has now disappeared. It will, therefore, be necessary to continue and to conclude separate alliances, inasmuch as the League admits its inability to offer a formal guarantee of protection to its own members." [10]

As a consequence of the disillusionment with the generality of Article 10 which left each state without specific guarantees, a twofold reaction emerged: "a determination to constitute regional understandings to strengthen by particular treaties the territorial security of individual states, and utilization of such agencies to free [states] from the obligations assumed under Article 10 by abstention in the participation of sanctions when they deemed that such sanctions were not in their best interests." [11]

The weakening of the obligation to preserve the territorial integrity of the members of the League led therefore to a search for alternative arrangements. It culminated in the proposal for a Draft Treaty of Mutual Assistance which in part constituted a return to regionalism. Under its provisions, which were submitted for approval to the members of the League in 1923, individual states could enter into "supplementary defensive agreements" that could be invoked subject to the risk of being condemned by the Council if wrongfully used. [12] While eighteen governments accepted the treaty in principle, the opposition of Great Britain and the dominions proved decisive and the treaty was rejected. In particular it was argued that the resort to bilateral security arrangements against third states might provide a convenient pretext for aggression in the name of self-defense, and that a subsequent finding of aggression by the Council could not be effectively implemented because "the Treaty required a unanimous vote of the Council before its judgement could go into effect . . ." [13]

An important attempt to strengthen the League developed with

the conclusion of the Locarno Agreements to preserve the status quo
of the Versailles peace settlement on the basis of regional security
commitments. These agreements attempted to provide a solution to
the most serious security problem of the era—the future status of the
Franco-German frontier. The Conference of Locarno ended in Decem-
berber, 1925 with the signature of a number of agreements, the most
important of which provided: [14]

I. A treaty of mutual guarantee of the Franco-German and Belgo-
German frontiers established by the Treaty of Versailles between
Germany, Belgium, France, Great Britain, and Italy, including the
permanent demilitarization of the Rhineland.

II. Peaceful settlement of all disputes arising between Belgium,
France, and Germany, including the conclusion of arbitration conventions between Germany and Belgium and Germany and France to
settle such disputes.

III. The renunication of war by Belgium, France and Germany except for self-defense.

While the agreements were not concluded under the auspices of the
League, they were placed under the control of the Council which was
to survey their execution. As a result of the Locarno Pacts, a sense
of "improved security arose which the British guarantee implanted
in the minds of Frenchmen and Germans that had an importance far
outweighing that of the question, whether . . . it would prove possible for Great Britain to fulfill her obligations." [15] The improvement
in international relations that resulted was instrumental in paving the
way for German membership in the League of Nations in 1926.

Unfortunately, the Locarno regional security system presupposed
a permanency in the European balance of power that was to break
down within ten years by the German violation of the demilitarized
zone of the Rhineland in March, 1936. France regarded the German
action as a flagrant violation of the Locarno agreements, but Great
Britain declined to resist this encroachment. In appraising the
Locarno system, E. H. Carr makes the following trenchant observation: [16] "In the long run, the Locarno Treaty was destructive both of
the Versailles Treaty and of the Covenant. It encouraged both the
view that the Versailles Treaty, unless confirmed by other engagements of a voluntary character, lacked binding force, and the view
that governments could not be expected to take military action in defense of frontiers in which they themselves were not directly interested."

The Little Entente. The Locarno Pacts were a set of regional agreements involving the major powers, but their ratification did not deter the conclusion of regional agreements among lesser powers since the Locarno agreements did not provide any guarantees for the frontiers of the newly created Central European states of Yugoslavia, Czechoslovakia, and Rumania who were also fearful of the possibility of German and particularly Hungarian aggression.

During 1920-1921 bilateral agreements between Czechoslovakia and Yugoslavia,Czechoslovakia and Rumania, and Rumania and Yugoslavia were concluded under which each state agreed to guarantee the territorial integrity of the other against aggression. They were initiated because these states feared that their frontiers were inadequately protected under Article 10 of the Covenant. They wished to insulate themselves as much as possible from great power domination and Hungarian efforts to restore the Hapsburg monarchy.[17] Elected to permanent membership on the League Council in 1923, the Little Entente powers, as they came to be known, thereby provided a basis for integrating their regional system into the League of Nations.

While France did not conclude formal political treaties with these states until 1925, "from the outset [there were] formal or informal military understandings . . . for the appointment of French military missions and for the supply of war material to the Little Entente armies." [18] At Geneva the Entente powers entered into close relations with France in the League. The basis for this early modus vivendi rested on a tacit agreement by which the smaller powers would aid France in the enforcement of the Versailles Treaty in return for which France would support the Little Entente against Hungary, and Yugoslavia in particular against Italy.[19] Thus the sphere of French vital security needs was widened beyond Germany into the Balkans in an attempt to perpetuate the territorial status quo of the 1919 peace settlement.

When the conciliatory spirit of Locarno began to disappear after Hitler's rise to power in 1933, the Little Entente powers moved into tighter cooperation by the signature of a new treaty whose object was "the complete unification of their general policies . . ." and the "establishment of an organization by which this common policy shall be directed." [20] A Permanent Council of Foreign Ministers, Permanent Secretariat, and an Economic Council were established to institutionalize their defensive alliance. Despite this cooperation, the Entente powers could not isolate their destiny from Austria and Hungary upon

whom they were dependent economically. With the decline of the
League of Nations under the vacillating and conciliatory policies of
England and France vis-a-vis Italy and Germany, the vulnerability
of the Little Entente increased and the association collapsed with the
Munich accord of 1938 which destroyed Czechoslovakia, the keystone
of the system, with the annexation of the Sudetenland by Germany.

In sum the Little Entente displayed all of the weaknesses of small
state regionalism: complete dependence upon a major power for
military security and military-political and socio-economic integration
of a low order. On the other hand, the Little Entente did demonstrate
the compatibility of universal and regional security systems. The
smaller powers maintained an unquestioned loyalty to the larger
organization during their period of membership and patterned a
treaty for the peaceful settlement of disputes after the League of Nations model treaty of conciliation and arbitration of 1928.

The Balkan Entente. Another example of small-state regionalism
during the inter-war period was the Balkan Entente, overlapping in its
membership with the Little Entente. Growing out of the Balkan
Pact of 1934, the arrangement was similar to the Little Entente in that
it was based on the principle of maintaining the territorial integrity of
the constituent members—Greece, Turkey, Rumania, and Yugoslavia.
They agreed to " . . . mutually guarantee the security of all their frontiers, to consult together on measures affecting their interests, [and]
not to embark on any political action towards a non-signatory Balkan
country without previous discussion." [21]

The basis for the participation of Yugoslavia and Rumania was the
fear of Bulgarian hostility, while for Greece and Turkey the arrangement served to unite two formerly implacable enemies. Unfortunately, the solidarity of the Entente became strained as a result of the divergent policies of Yugoslavia and Greece. Yugoslavia also viewed
the pact as a means of preventing Italian interference in the Balkans
while Greece attached a declaration to her ratification of the treaty
which renounced any obligation to engage in hostilities with a non-
Balkan power thereby cooling relations with Yugoslavia.[22] Subsequently, relations between Bulgaria and Yugoslavia improved and this
cancelled for Yugoslavia the usefulness of the Entente and isolated
her from the other member states.

Though the Balkan Entente survived the international crises of the early and middle 1930's, it was unable to resist the encroachment of German aggression which victimized all of the member states.

The Inter-American System. No discussion of regionalism between 1920 and 1945 would be complete without mention of the inter-American system of cooperation. Although susceptible to periods of disunity, it was the most advanced regional system of the inter-war period and figured prominently in the discussions at the San Francisco Conference in 1945 regarding the relations between the United Nations and regional agencies.[23]

The inter-American system originated in the latter quarter of the nineteenth century out of a common historical tradition: all of the member states attained their independence by virtue of revolutions against imperial control. This is not to deny, however, the very great divergencies of economic development and political stability within the region.

Until the formation of the Organization of American States in 1948, which pulled together in one organization the various activities of the inter-American system, continuity was maintained chiefly by means of periodic international conferences dealing with major economic, political, and cultural affairs. During the period between 1923-1938 an inter-American conference system developed. Numerous treaties were concluded among the members, involving in addition to technical subjects a formidable juridical structure for the peaceful settlement of disputes.

With the rise of Nazism and the threat that it posed to Latin America, the conference system was supplemented by a series of Foreign Ministers meetings held between 1938 and 1942 in which the member states began planning joint measures for the defense of the hemisphere, culminating in the Declaration of Havana of 1940 under which an attack by a non-American state in Latin America was considered an act of aggression against all those states signing the declaration.

Although the early Pan-American movement was in a sense a corrective to the unilateralism of the Monroe Doctrine and the supremacy of the United States, relations between the "Colossus of the North" and the smaller states to the south were complicated by the American imperialism of the first quarter of the twentieth century that retarded a closer cooperation within the region. The establishment of the Good Neighbor policy by President Roosevelt in 1933 was an attempt to remove the stigma of interventionism from the United States and thereby eliminate what had been the most objectionable factor in inter-American relations. Acceptance by the United States of the principle of non-intervention under the Buenos Aires Convention of 1936 marked the legal and political affirmation of a new stage in hemispheric relations.

Insofar as relations with the League of Nations were concerned, however, the developing regionalization in the Western Hemisphere operated outside the control and influence of the universal organization. This was caused not only by the failure of the United States to join the League and thereby establish a connecting link to coordinate the universal and regional structures, but also because for all practical purposes the League excluded the Western Hemisphere from the purview of its operations in deference to Article 21 of the Covenant. Commenting on the relationship, Professor Charles Martin observed that[24] "Mr. Cordell Hull, the architect of the "Good Neighbor Policy," desired only such League of Nations cooperation as would not complicate or involve the integrity of the American organization of nations. Any League of Nations connections were quite nebulous. The influence and impact of the League, as a universal institution, on the Western Hemisphere, were negligible."

Despite the absence of coordinating links, there were few evidences of conflict between the two systems. In the Grand Chaco dispute between Bolivia and Paraguay in 1928 the Council asserted the right to investigate but subsequently relinquished consideration to enable the United States and several Latin American countries to function as mediators. It did not, however, fail to act but sent an emphatic reminder to the two parties of their obligations as Members of the League; warned them against any military action which might aggravate the situation; [and] requested its President to keep in touch with events and call it together in special session if further fighting should occur . . ."[25]

Prompt action by the Council brought a quick reply from the disputants who assured that they would abide by their obligations under the Covenant and subsequently accepted the good offices of the Pan-American Arbitration Conference.[26] A Commission of Inquiry and Conciliation formed in Washington in January, 1929, consisting of five neutral American states and the disputants, succeeded in settling the immediate controversy without, resolving the dispute.[27] It was later reported that the action of the Council had averted a major deterioration of the situation.

However, four years later hostilities between the two nations resumed and the League again became directly involved when Paraguay appealed to the Council.

After efforts to establish a truce failed, the dispute was transferred to the League Assembly which ordered an arms embargo[28] but "the . . . assembly did not take stronger action because of the opposition of . . . Argentina, Chile, Peru, and Uruguay, and later handed over the problem to the nations of that continent for solution. The danger of conflicting with the Pan-American peace machinery led to caution . . ."

The Grand Chaco dispute clearly revealed that a lack of coordination between the regional and universal organizations complicated the solution of the controversy. If mediation was hampered because of the intransigence of Bolvia and Paraguay, it was also weakened by the weakly coordinated efforts of neighboring states, the other American republics, and the League.[29] Fortunately, this was the only serious instance of conflict between the inter-American and universal systems during the inter-war period.

Summary. The preceding survey of regionalism under the League of Nations discloses certain tendencies that will now be summarized. While the inter-war period revealed a periodic fluctuation between universalism and regionalism, no marked disequilibrium between the two forms of cooperation developed. Despite the failure of the principle of collective security, the League of Nations remained the dominant international instrumentality for peace and security with the Little Entente, Balkan Entente, and Inter-American systems subordinate and supplementary adjuncts. If the vagueness of the Covenant prompted a search for alternatives to fill in the gaps of the universal system, establishment of subsidiary regional security agencies failed to produce any greater degree of political, military, or economic effectiveness than the wider framework of which they were a part.

Both the universal organization and its regional supplements were weakened by the lack of explicit legal and constitutional provisions for coordination in the Covenant. More fundamentally, international organizations could not escape the influence of the major centrifugal force of the inter-war period: the world wide economic depression and the subsequent trend to economic nationalism; the failure of the leading architect of the Covenant, the United States, to join the League;

the inability of the major powers to solve the dilemma of security
versus disarmament; failure of Britain and France and the other leading members of the League to act resolutely to meet the aggressions
of Japan, Italy, and Germany; and especially the general reluctance
of all nations to subordinate national sovereignty and national interest into a wider universal framework of international cooperation.

In assessing the deterioration in world order from 1919 to 1934,
Professor Carleton J. H. Hayes observed that[30] "efforts without preced-
ent were made during the fifteen years from 1919 to 1934 to establish
a new world-order of national security and international peace. Never
before had there been such an invention and elaboration of peace
machinery—League of Nations, World Court, International Labor
Office, mutual security pacts, international conventions. Nevertheless, it must be equally apparent that all this peace machinery did not
actually prevent war or create a sense of security, and that at the end
of the fifteen years the new world-order was still not a reality but only
a dissolving dream."

Hayes attributes this breakdown to an intensification of nationalism:
"Peace machinery existed, but its successful operation required an
effective will not only of idealistic statesmen and intellectuals but of
the masses in the several countries . . . It required a public opinion
within every nation favorable to the subordination of national interest
and policy to international adjustment. This, however, was significantly lacking. On the contrary, the bulk of public opinion in every
country, instead of keeping pace with the development of peace
machinery and becoming more internationalist, grew ever more nationalist, more devoted to the concept of national honor, the defense
of national rights, and the unrestrained pursuit of national interests."

The various experiments in small-state regionalism demonstrated
that legal guarantees for mutual assistance in the event of aggression
were unlikely to be effective unles they were supported by concrete
defense forces. Moreover, the concentration of international politics
in Europe during the inter-war period proved the impossibility of excluding the influence of major powers from these agencies.

The Little Entente depended for its viability on the support of
France while the Balkan Entente was divided over the relations of its
members to the major powers outside the Balkan area. Except for
the inter-American system whose accelerating unity was often offset
by hostility of the smaller members toward the United States, the
other regional systems were unable to expand their essentially negative

function of defense into more than modest degrees of positive institutional cooperation. In neither the Little Entente or the Balkan Entente did the members succeed in developing any cohesive economic or military unity since the fate of each arrangement was dependent upon geographically adjacent non-member states:[31] "no scheme for Central-Eastern European integration could overcome the contradiction of a political orientation against the German Reich and economic dependence on the German market and product."

Ultimately, the small powers were not able to isolate their destiny from that of the League of Nations whose failure to halt aggression signaled the collapse of both regional and universal security.

The Western Hemisphere provided an example of the type of confusion that may ensue from the vague constitutional arrangement between universalism and regionalism contained in the Covenant. Virtual exemption of the Western Hemisphere from the control of the League and the failure of the United States to join the universal organization contributed to uncertainty in the handling of inter-American disputes. A paradoxical desire of the members of the League to refrain from alienating the United States combined with assertion of the right to apply the Covenant in Latin America created confusion, weakening the assumption that regional systems may reduce the number of disputes that reach the universal organization through their own superior peaceful settlement procedures. Failure of the inter-American system to settle the Grand Chaco dispute until 1938 revealed the limitations of the regional approach to peaceful settlement.

Regionalism in the Western Hemisphere, however, was more progressive than in Europe because the member states were relatively isolated from the major power struggles of the era. They were thus freer to develop geographic proximity and a common political ideology into a tighter legal and political solidarity especially after the United States accepted the principle of non-intervention in the internal affairs of the member states. Achievement in the Western Hemisphere of a highly advanced juridical structure for the peaceful settlement of disputes, a periodic conference system to discuss common problems, and a network of treaties regulating various economic and social matters must be viewed as the most significant accomplishment of regional cooperation during the inter-war period.

It was principally the future of the inter-American system that was to concern the leading Latin American statesmen at the San Francisco Conference where the nations assembled to draw up a constitution for a new universal organization. Fearing that the new organization might be dominated by the great power complex that emerged in 1945, they led the fight for constitutional legitimacy of regionalism of considerably greater scope than in the Covenant. It is to this development that we now turn for a fuller appreciation of the legal and political aspects of regionalism and universalism following World War II.

Chapter IV

REGIONALISM AND THE UNITED NATIONS CHARTER

The preceding chapter discussed the major aspects of the relations between universal and regional organization during the period between World War I and World War II. It forms a necessary background to the discussion that follows concerning the methods by which the successor organization to the League attempted to reconcile regionalism and universalism more explicitly than in 1920. Equilibrium between universalism and regionalism depended upon a more specific responsibility for peace and security by the major powers after 1945. It was assumed that the wartime cooperation of the great powers would continue within the new international organization in which they would have prevailing power for the enforcement of peace. Regional arrangements were to function as supplementary adjuncts of the United Nations. The primary responsibility of the great powers for maintaining peace was reflected in their permanent membership on the Security Council and in the rule of their unanimity on all important Council action.

In addition, the Charter recognized the existence of regionalism in a manner more detailed and thorough than the vagueness of Article 21 of the Covenant. An entire chapter was devoted to the relations between regional security agencies and the United Nations. Though Articles 51, 52, 53, and 54 have been the object of numerous analyses since 1945 and the material which follows is no more than a succinct summary of the conflicting interpretations with a modest reinterpretation by the author, detailed examination of the constitutional theory of the Charter is essential for historical perspective as well as for demonstrating the ways in which the theoretical reconciliation of universalism and regionalism has been vitiated by subsequent political events.

When the San Francisco Conference convened in June, 1945 to draft a constitution for a new general international organization, representatives of the inter-American system and the recently formed League of Arab States were concerned about the relationship between the new organization and their regional associations.[1] In fact the concern was manifest earlier after the dissemination of the Dumbarton Oaks proposals in late 1944.[2] Uncertainties arose over the fact that the Dumbarton Oaks proposals contemplated a modest role for regionalism by stipulating that while regional agencies might be utilized by the Security Council for enforcement purposes ". . . no enforcement action was to be taken under regional arrangements or by regional agencies without the authorization of the Security Council."[3]

With the clarification of voting procedures in the Council reached at Yalta in February, 1945 under which unanimity of the five major powers was required for enforcement action against an aggressor, a situation could arise in which one member of the Council could block approval for sanctions action contemplated under a regional system. Such action was contemplated in the adoption of the Act of Chapultepec in March, 1945 under which the inter-American nations sought to strengthen their bonds of mutual security by developing a commitment of collective assistance to any member whose territory was violated by aggression. It was this announcement which " . . . brought to the fore the issue of how such a regional system was to be fitted into a general global system with sufficient assurance that the operation of the regional system would not be thwarted at every turn by states outside the Hemisphere."[4]

In addition to the problem of reconciling the Inter-American system with the United Nations, there was the possibility that the Security Council itself might prove ineffective to deal with threats to the peace and/or acts of aggression because of the time required for concerted action. Awareness of this possibility was voiced by the French delegate to the Conference, Joseph Paul-Boncourt: [5]

"My country has complete confidence in the system of collective security, in the Security Council, in the Charter which we are making . . . But whatever precautions may be taken in the various committees, in order to assure swift and effective action by the Security Council, it is impossible to prevent delays resulting from its meetings, its discussion, from the transport from countries often distant of material and men assigned to those who are attacked. And this, coupled with the lightning rapidity which aggression in modern war is capable of, may defeat—still more in any future war if that unhappily should occur—may subject a country to the risk of death. . . ."

The French attitude was also shared by the British (concerned over their responsibilities to the Commonwealth) and the Latin American and Arab states. It led to sharp debate at the Conference that culminated in proposals to modify the Dumbarton Oaks draft to permit greater autonomy for regional systems.[6] As a result of these discussions Article 51 was inserted into the Charter, stipulating that "Nothing in the present Charter shall impair the inherent right of individual or collective self-defense if an armed attack occurs against a Member of the United Nations, until the Security Council has taken the measures necessary to maintain international peace and security. . . ."

This article was included, however, under Chapter VII (Action with Respect to Threats to the Peace) rather than under Chapter VIII (Regional Arrangements) since inclusion under the latter would have precluded enforcement action independent of the Security Council.[7]

There are, however, ambiguities in the article. Self-defensive measures have always been sanctioned under customary international law, but under what circumstances may they be employed as exceptions to the general prohibition against the use of force in the Charter? In particular, the article established no criteria for distinguishing between self-defense and aggression in the event of an armed attack and therefore did not preclude the possibility of aggressive action by states under the guise of self-defense. In such instances it would be unlikely that the regional agency involved would withdraw and yield control over the action to the Security Council. Even if it is admitted that effort to separate measures of self-defense from measures of aggression is an impossible task, the dominant role of the Security Council is weakened by the autonomy granted to regional agencies under Article 51. In the only instance in which the article was invoked by a regional agency, the Arab League in connection with Israel, that agency later deferred to the Security Council and entered into cease-fire negotiations. But the possibility of a future clash is not entirely academic.

Conversely, the right of collective self-defense has been defended in the event the Security Council may be deadlocked when an armed attack occurs.[8] In view of the paralysis that developed in the Council after 1945, the collective self-defense provision of Article 51 was to take on added meaning as newly formed regional agencies attempted to justify their consistency with the United Nations Charter by citing the right of collective self-defense. Whether Article 51 permitted regional action in advance of an armed attack was ignored. A literal reading of the article indicates that collective self-defense is legal only after an armed attack. On the other hand, successful collective self-defense may be difficult without prior planning and organization of regional systems. Such strategic considerations underlie many arguments against a literal interpretation.

Article 51 has provided a legal escape clause for the justification of numerous collective self-defense agencies without any provision for their control by the Security Council in the event of an armed attack. The situation has been well described by Professor Julius Stone: [9]

"The use of Article 51 shows itself . . . as the frontier for the moment reached between the traditional anarchic international system, and the real collective security system projected in the Charter . . . The alignments of States in the North Atlantic Treaty and related organizations, and in the series of mutual assistance treaties sponsored by the Soviet Union, could fight a war to the bitter end, under the title of self-defense, without a determination by the Security Council [because of the veto] of the legality of either side's conduct . . . or any effective Security Council measures to end the war. To this extent 'self-defense' under Article 51 has reoccupied the field of the Security Council as a collective peace-enforcing agency."

Regional Arrangements. As noted in the preceding chapter, the experience of the inter-war period disclosed a minimum of direct antagonism between the various regional understandings and the League of Nations. Collapse of the universal approach to peace and security may be attributed to the unwillingness of the leading members of the League of Nations to endorse the requirements of collective security rather than to the existence of a number of regional organizations.

Despite the failure of universal collective security under the League, the prevailing sentiment at the San Francisco Conference favored a return to universalism. It was expressed through provisions in the Charter giving to the Security Council dominant responsibility for enforcing peace and security subject, however, to the loophole at Article 51. Yet Article 51 failed to satisfy the demands of the Latin American states, the Arab League, and the British Commonwealth for a more explicit recognition of regionalism. As a result of such pressures, a separate chapter in the Charter specifically legitimized regional arrangements. It amounted to a compromise between the "theoretical preference for universalism and political pressures for regionalism." [30] If the compromise is somewhat vague because the Charter is silent concerning the means by which regional arrangements were to be controlled by the United Nations, the provisions of Chapter VIII reflected a realistic recognition of the utility of such arrangements as well as the desirability of assigning them a role subordinate to the universal organization.

Article 52 specifically recognized regional arrangements as ancillary devices for insuring peace and security on the regional level as well as in the pacific settlement of regional disputes. Acceptance of such arrangements arose not only because of political pressures generated by various regional groups, but was also based on the following theoretical considerations: [11]

(1) ". . . national interest and national capacity to exercise power effectively are to an important extent determined, even in the era of air communications and travel, by geographical location. . . ."

(2) "in the historical evolution of international organization for peace and security, emphasis has been placed on cooperation between those [states] similarly situated with respect to interests which are to be served by such arrangements."

Unfortunately, the Charter does not define the meaning of regional arrangements except to imply that they exist primarily for the purpose of safeguarding international peace and security. As a result of the silence of the Charter, confusion has arisen over the question as to whether such agencies as NATO, SEATO, and CENTO are collective self-defense agencies under Article 51, regional arrangements or both.

Although the Egyptian delegation to the San Francisco Conference suggested an amendment to the effect that "regional arrangements should be established only among states which constitute a natural, geographic, cultural or historical group," it was rejected "because many states desired to include as regional arrangements groups of a purely political or military character . . ." [12] In practical usage, the term has been used to denote political or military groupings, but it was also recognized at the Conference that it is susceptible to economic and social connotations. [13] Because of the many ways in which regionalism may manifest itself, precise formulation may not be desirable. But if one takes this position, then the problem of differentiating regional arrangements from collective self-defense arrangements still remains.

Under Article 52 (2) "the Members of the United Nations entering into such arrangements or constituting such agencies shall make every effort to achieve pacific settlement of local disputes through such arrangements or by such regional agencies before referring them to the Security Council." This clause reflects the view that regional agencies may have purposes other than military security: they may serve to ameliorate conflicts by peaceful means before violence erupts and thus be useful supplements to the United Nations peaceful settlement machinery. When this clause is read in conjunction with Article 33 of the Charter which exhorts states to exhaust all other peaceful settlement devices before submitting disputes to the United Nations, it will be seen that regional agencies are to have priority with regard to the settlement of those disputes of a purely regional character.[14]

In this connection it is difficult to agree with the view that Article 33 constitutes a neutralization of the authority of the universal organ in the pacific settlement of international disputes.[15] It could be argued that the article is necessary for both quantitative and qualitative considerations: quantitatively, it may serve as a check on the tendency to overburden the Security Council with disputes that could be solved without its intercession; qualitatively, it envisages submission to the Council of only those disputes which have not proved amenable to mediation, conciliation, diplomacy, adjudication, or regional settlement. In such serious cases, the Security Council may legitimately exercise its authority to issue recommendations to the disputants under Articles 34 and 35 of the Charter.

The Charter therefore provides for the harmonization of regional and universal systems of pacific settlement by integrating the regional into the universal framework without jeopardizing the autonomy of the former or the preponderant role of the latter should the regional system fail to be effective.

Under Article 53 regional agencies are further integrated into the universal organization as subordinate adjuncts to the United Nations in the enforcement of peace and security: "The Security Council shall, where appropriate, utilize such regional arrangements or agencies for enforcement action under its authority. But no enforcement action shall be taken . . . without the authorization of the Security Council, with the *exception* of measures against any enemy state . . . until such time as the Organization may, on request of the Governments concerned, be charged with the responsibility for preventing further aggression by such a state."

This exception was included because it was agreed that the Organization was not to be responsible for working out or enforcing the peace settlement that would follow World War II.[16] It would be theoretically possible for collective security action to be taken by regional agencies outside of the control of the Security Council if such action was directed against ex-enemy states, pursuant to the provisions of Article 107. Professor Stone has aptly characterized the potentally dangerous situation that could develop on the basis of this exception:[17]

"Article 107 and the exception in Article 53 seemed of transistory and merely precautionary importance in 1945; but two developments have now converted them into a potential escape clause from the main obligations of the Charter. The first is the estrangement between the Soviet Union and the other permanent members of the Security Council; the other is the consequential division of Germany into the Western-sponsored West German Federal Republic on the one hand, and the Soviet-sponsored East German People's Republic on the other. This division makes it likely that in any hostilities which might arise between the Soviet Union and the Western States, each could plausibly allege that its action was directed under Article 53, paragraph 1, against "a renewal of aggressive policy" by an ex-enemy (a German) State, fighting on the other side; or was "action . . . taken as a result of" the Second World War under Article 107. Each side could, therefore, lawfully organize what are really alliances against the other under the license to act against ex-enemy states."

Finally, the provision of Article 53 prohibiting enforcement action by regional agencies unless sanctioned by the Security Council has been effectively nullified by Article 51. Even if such agencies were willing to act on behalf of the Council in areas not involving their own vital interests, the contemporary impasse in the Council could prevent their action if either the United States or the Soviet Union chose to exercise a veto.[18] Thus the subordination of regional arrangements envisaged in Article 53 may be blocked in three ways: by invocation of the right of collective-self-defense under Article 51; by justifying independent action on the basis of the exception permitted by Article 53 against ex-enemy states; as ancillary enforcement agencies they could be prevented from taking action by any major power in the Security Council.

Article 54 concluded Chapter VIII on Regional Arrangements and further emphasized the subsidiary character of regional agencies: "The Security Council shall at all times be kept fully informed of activities undertaken or in contemplation under regional arrangements

or by regional agencies for the maintenance of international peace
and security." But there was silence on its implementation. Osten-
sibly, the Committee which framed the article expected that the
coordination of such activities would not involve any difficulties,
relying on the good faith of such agencies to furnish information on
their activities to the Council.[10] However, most of the major regional security agencies established since 1945 base their legality on
the right of collective self-defense under Article 51 instead of regional arrangements under Chapter VIII. As a result they are required to inform the Council only after and not in advance of
military action.

As a consequence of the failure of the Charter to specify more
fully the means by which regional arrangements would be controlled
by the United Nations, the theoretical compromise reached at San
Francisco has been undermined by the tendency of regional arrangement and/or collective self-defense agencies to assert the widest
autonomy in the conduct of their activities. Even if the assumption
of great power harmony had been achieved after 1945, regional
agencies may have attempted to take advantage of the vagueness
of the Charter provisions for coordinating regionalism and universalism.

The deficiencies of the Charter provisions on regional arrangements have been appropriately noted: [20] "The Charter provided no
formal procedure whereby regional arrangements could be brought
into relationship with the United Nations. These were wholly independent legal entities. To be sure, the Charter entreated, in fact
obligated, adherents to regional arrangments to conduct themselves
in accordance with the principles of the United Nations. Only as
they did so would any regional arrangement function within the
framework of the United Nations."

Collective Self-Defense and the Charter. We move now to an
examination of a difficult legal and political question that developed
in the years following the San Francisco Conference and continues
to be debated. What is the distinction between collective self-
defense arrangements sanctioned under Article 51 and regional arrangements operating under Chapter VIII of the Charter? Although the
confusion would have been reduced if the Security Council had been
able to function harmoniously and thereby deter the proliferation of
regional agencies based on Article 51, its inability to do so raises

an important and controversial problem of constitutional interpretation.

One possible interpretation is that Article 51 was designed to permit the ad hoc organization of collective force to meet specific situations rather than to be the basis for the establishment of permanent security organizations, provision for which is made in Chapter VIII. As a result of the fact that Article 51 has been cited as the legal basis for such agencies, they have been able to escape all regulation and control by the Security Council. While such control would have obviously interfered with their efficacy because of the veto power of the Soviet Union, this does not alter the view that they fall more properly under Chapter VIII than under Article 51.[21] Such an interpretation appears valid if collective self-defense ". . . means the right of every Member (of the United Nations) to consider an armed attack against another member as being equivalent to an attack against itself and to take any measures required to repel such an attack."[22] The existence of prior regional defense agreements may be desirable but not essential, for the definition implies the possibility of spontaneous multilateral action to defeat aggression. This is the view of collective self-defense taken by the authors of an authoritative commentary on the Charter:[23]

"The collective action under Article 51 need not be under the terms of a formal agreement. There is nothing in the Charter or in the record of discussions at San Francisco that excludes the possibility of action by two or more states, without any definite commitment in advance on the basis of common interest in meeting successfully a common danger. In fact, in thus safeguarding the right of collective self-defense the Article provides the opportunity for Members of the United Nations to act together in self-defense if any armed attack occurs . . . [presumably because the Security Council has failed to act]."

Professor Stone has argued that the essence of regional arrangements under Artcles 52 and 53 is the maintenance of international peace and security within rather than between regions.[24] And yet we are confounded by the fact that the most important regional security arrangements established since 1945 apparently do not fit this assumption since they were not based on the possibility of intra-regional aggression but as protection against the threat of extra-regional attack. If Professor Stone is correct in his interpretation of regional arrangements for the maintenance of regional peace, however, it would be appropriate to note that conditions do not permit such a restrictive interpretation in practice.

Regional agencies cannot isolate themselves from the wider world of which they are a part as the experience of all major systems under the League of Nations and United Nations reveals. Such experience indicates that regional security agreements have been established as defenses against the possibility of external rather than internal aggression. To view the situation otherwise would be to postulate a static condition of international politics in which regional entities would be permanently insulated from extra-regional influences. Because of the globalization of world politics since 1945, regional entities are more susceptible to such influences. Thus to define regional arrangements solely as instruments for the maintenance of regional peace and security seems unduly restrictive.

The major reason for excluding NATO, SEATO, and CENTO as regional arrangements, however, lies not in the increasing influence of extra-regional forces but in the independence of such agencies from United Nations control as envisaged under Chapter VIII of the Charter. But this raises the question of the nature of such agencies? If they are incompatible with the principles of Chapter VIII, does that mean that they are therefore legal as collective self-defense arrangements under Article 51? While a majority of writers would reply in the affirmative, this does not exclude the possibility of another viewpoint.

The Charter implies that regional arrangements formed subsequent to the establishment of the United Nations should be legally integrated into the universal system instead of being autonomous of it. If Article 51 justifies the right of individual and collective self-defense, it does not sanction the right of nations to form self-defense agencies independent of United Nations control which is clearly the situation today. Rather, as argued earlier, Article 51 could be interpreted as permitting only the spontaneous mobilization of collective force. Chapter VIII is the more logical legal basis of permanent regional security agencies. If it be objected that the establishment of Western security systems on the basis of Article 51 was an unavoidable response to a paralyzed universal system, this does not alter the conclusion that their freedom from control by the United Nations is contrary to the spirit and letter of the Charter.

As suggested, a possible rationalization for the contemporary disequilibrium between universalism and regionalism may be found in Article 1 (1) of the Charter under which the United Nations is "to take effective collective measures for the prevention and removal of threats to the peace, and for the suppression of acts of aggression or other breaches of the peace. . . ." If the United Nations is immobilized as a result of the failure of the great powers to unite on matters of peace and security and if the General Assembly can fill in this vacuum under the Uniting for Peace Resolution only in a recommendatory manner, then it may be argued that collective self-defense agencies are the only alternatives to international anarchy since they may operate instantaneously and unconditionally. While this argument has obvious merit, the substitution of uncontrolled regional action for an inoperative collective security system is an inadequate solution to the problem of world order.

Often referred to inaccurately as collective security agencies, regional systems represent two deviations from the Wilsonian concept: they are geographically limited segments of the universalism implicit in the theory and are directed toward specific enemy states rather than designed to repel aggression impartially.[25] As Professor Stone has observed, ". . . the invocation of 'collective self-defence' as a residual obligation of Members under Article 1, paragraph 1, cannot conceal the fact that 'collective self-defence' comes not to fulfill the Charter, but because . . . the Charter remains unfulfilled."[26]

A NOTE ON REINTEGRATION OF REGIONAL AGENCIES INTO THE UNITED NATIONS SYSTEM

Is the contemporary imbalance between universalism and regionalism irreversible or are there any possibilities for a restoration of the constitutional compromise developed in the Charter? A recent authoritative study of proposals for reform of the United Nations suggested three remedies for increasing the control of the United Nations over regional arrangements:[27]

"(1) If the United Nations objects to any provision of a regional arrangement, members of the organization should modify it to the satisfaction of the UN.

"(2) If a regional organization takes action that it believes is required to ensure the defense of its members, but the United Nations finds differently and directs the regional group to cease action, it should comply.

"(3) If the United Nations recommends that a regional agency be utilized, the agency should accept a particular assignment. If, however, the United Nations becomes dissatisfied with the action of the regional agency, the United Nations should be able to halt the action."

All of these suggestions presuppose a more centralized and unified universal organization than now exists or is likely to exist for some time. Moreover, inasmuch as the majority of regional agencies purport to be based on Article 51 rather than Chapter VIII, these suggestions would affect only a very few regional arrangements.

More specifically, the difficulties involved in a restoration of the constitutional compromise of the Charter stem from a combination of political and legal considerations. Legally, reintegration is complicated because of the differences in the character of the obligations assumed under the United Nations and those assumed under existing regional agreements; the former relies on conditional obligations which require the unanimity of the great powers for enforcement action while most regional defense agreements permit unconditional sanctions action against aggression. [28]

A more fundamental difficulty has been suggested by Professor Stanley Hoffmann: "the states that have consented to the important sacrifice of powers with respect to regional organizatons do not have the material or legal means to consent to additional [sacrifices] for the benefit of a renovated United Nations: they cannot serve two masters; under the League the only states ready to consent to extended sacrifices . . . were those which could only count on the [universal] organization for their protection; but the multiplication of regional agreements tends to protect all the small states: they have therefore less need of turning toward the United Nations." [29]

While there may be plausibility in the present reluctance of the superpowers to strengthen the United Nations at the expense of their own regional systems, the situation may be different for small states.

It is in the interest of the smaller states to strengthen the world organization since it cannot be assumed that the multiplication of regional security systems has promoted or increased the peace and security of the world by maintaining a delicate "balance of terror." If anything, they have exacerbated world tension to such an extent that some of the smaller members of Western blocs have begun to question their advantages in an era in which rival alliances increasingly confront each other with destructive nuclear power. Even if it is granted that small states gain a degree of protective security from such arrangements, the same assumption cannot be ventured for the great number of uncommitted or non-aligned nations that have emerged since 1945. Most of these states view the conflicting regional alignments with concern and trepidation fearful of the consequences of regional autonomy from the United Nations. In such circumstances, and recognizing that nuclear war would not leave them untouched, the smaller nations have consistently supported a revitalized United Nations system which could more adequately regulate contemporary regional security systems.

More plausible as an obstacle to the reintegration of regional systems is Professor Hoffmann's contention that Soviet and American blocs are so fundamentally antagonistic that they cannot be reconciled under the same roof. [30] If contemporary antagonisms could be resolved, regional defense agencies might then revert to the more modest role contemplated for them in the Charter. If this were to materialize, it is conceivable that their unconditional obligations to assist attacked states might be amended to permit the United Nations to function as the institution with primary responsibility for peace and security.

Thus, the most serious obstacle impeding a reintegration of regional alliances into the United Nations is not the smaller nations but the two superpowers. An assessment of the possibilities for reintegration therefore involves a consideration of whether and if the current bipolarization of world politics may be ameliorated. Unless and until there is a softening of the antagonisms that pervade the regional bloc systems of these powers, it is unlikely that the contemporary disequilibrium between universalism and regionalism will be corrected. This problem will be more fully explored toward the conclusion of this study.

CHAPTER V

THE GROWTH OF REGIONAL ORGANIZATIONS

To comprehend fully the contemporary relationship between universal and regional organization, the complex political, economic, and military factors that fostered the trend toward regionalism after 1945 must be examined. Unlike the corresponding period following World War I, the aftermath of the Allied victory over Germany and Japan saw a surprisingly rapid disintegration of hopes for a new world order. The subsequent emergence of regional agencies to fill in the void only superficially resembled a similar trend toward regionalism after 1920.

The new regionalism in the West was directed against the expansionism of a former wartime ally, while regional agreements initiated under the League of Nations were designed to prevent the recurrence of aggression by former enemy states.[1] Disillusionment with the ideal of collective security under universal auspices became so intense as a result of the schism among the great powers that regional security agencies developed as substitutes for rather than complements of the universal security system envisioned in the United Nations Charter. Under the League of Nations regional agencies were established as supplemental systems rather than as replacements for the universal organization. The reaction after 1945 was a pragmatic response to the changing dynamics of international politics rather than on the conviction that regionalism was theoretically superior to universalism as a method of international cooperation.

In this chapter we will explore the circumstances which precipitated the flight from universalism and consider not only the rise of regional security agencies but also the various experiments in regional economic and social cooperation established after 1945. The relationship of these functional agencies to the deteriorating international order will be assessed in conjunction with other factors that have influenced regionalism in Western Europe, Latin America, the Middle East, the Far East, and Africa. For example, the growth of regional functionalism may be viewed in part as a response to the "decline of the territorial state" created by rapidly changing scientific and technological conditions that have rendered the state more penetrable and less secure than at any other period in modern history.[2]

Of major significance is the extent to which regional agencies constitute a movement away from exclusive reliance on the nation-state as the basic unit of international relations. It will therefore be necessary to analyze the difficult problem of political integration in relation to economic and social integration as well as to consider the tangible and intangible prerequisites necessary for a cohesive regionalism.

The discussion begins with an analysis of the forces which prompted the proliferation of Western and Soviet security arrangements. In 1957 Professor Ernst Haas reported that 58 of the then 81 member states of the United Nations belonged to at least one of the nine major regional alliances, which gives some idea as to the importance which member states attached to regionalism as an approach to security.[3] This figure would have undoubtedly been higher if it were not for the existence of a large bloc of newly independent nations that eschewed membership in military alliances. What were the circumstances that brought such alliances into being? To what extent have they flowered into genuine regional communities with goals transcending the objectives that led to their creation? What is the nature of the conflicts that have arisen within such alliances and between the alliances and the United Nations? Each of these questions need to be probed if we are to obtain a clearer perception of the advantages and limitations of contemporary regional security systems.

It is customary to attribute the growth of regional security agencies to the emergence of Soviet imperialism after 1945 revealed through territorial aggrandizement in Eastern Europe, noncooperation in the Security Council, intransigency over the signing of the various postwar peace treaties, and generally hostile attitudes toward the West. Such explanations, however, are incomplete without an appreciation of the fundamental changes in the international power structure which confronted the world in 1945 and contributed in part to intense bipolar rivalry in and out of the United Nations, blocking the restoration of universal order.

Given the nature of power disparity in the modern state system peace must always rest on some minimum degree of consensus among the most powerful states. Such a consensus pervaded the era of Pax Britannica of the 19th century, but the prospects for such consensus and stability were much less in 1945 than in 1815. In the earlier period the existence of a complex balance of power involving several states of approximately equal power, supplemented by the stabilizing feature of the "balancer" power role of Great Britain, were

major contributions to political order. To these factors must be added
the fact that the instrumentalities of warfare utilized during the
period were not capable of totally obliterating states involved in hostilities, thereby insuring their legal and political continuity once
peace was restored. In the period since 1945 drastic increases in the
destructive capabilities of new weapons unleashed through the discovery of nuclear fission threatens if not the extinction of the state
system then its modification into a collectivity under the hegemonic
influence of the superpowers. Finally, the ideological consensus that
pervaded Europe in the nineteenth century and mitigated frequent
disturbances of the status quo has been replaced by an intense ideological dissensus that complicates the attainment of international
order and stability.

After 1945 the structure of the balance of power had so altered
that peace no longer depended on a consensus among several powers
but upon only two, the United States and the Soviet Union, confronting each other in a "tight" bipolar balance of power system.
Regardless of the consequent ideological rift that rendered a universal
order so precarious, amicable relations even among two states that
shared a common ideology would have been subject to severe strain.
The bipolar structure of power would have made them potential if
not actual competitors since no third state or group of states existed
to act as a "balancer" in any conflict that might arise.

While the change in the balance of power helps to explain the
difficulty of restoring universalism, perhaps the most important cause
for failure lay in the increasing ideological conflict and competition
between the United States and the Soviet Union manifested in and
out of the United Nations. The assumption that these powers would
cooperate to maintain the peace rested in turn on another assumption:
that they shared a common view of what was to be defended or
what constituted the territorial status quo. When it soon appeared
that there were divergent interpretations of the status quo as disclosed by Soviet expansion in Eastern Europe and attempts to engulf
Western Europe as well, all hopes for a universal order under the aegis
of the United Nations began to fade. It became apparent that
international organization for peace and security could not be divorced
from the dynamics of international politics which set limits on what
the United Nations could achieve.

Repeated exercise of the veto by the Soviet Union in the Security
Council, its menacing attitude toward Iran in 1946, and a generally

uncooperative behavior over the signing of the post-war peace treaties prompted the United States and its European allies to search for alternatives to a system of universal peace and security. It led to the introduction in June, 1948, of a resolution by Senator Arthur Vandenberg urging the following objectives:[4]

"(1) Progressive development of regional and other collective arrangements for individual and collective self-defense in accordance with the purposes, principles, and provisions of the (United Nations) Charter.

"(2) Association of the United States . . . with such regional and other collective arrangements as are based on continuous and effective self-help and mutual aid, and as effect its national security."

The approval of the Vandenberg resolution by the Senate reflected a pragmatic response of the United States to a rapidly deteriorating international climate. Subsequent establishment of mutual security arrangements with the nations Western Europe, the Far East, the Pacific, and indirectly the Middle East was the institutional and political embodiment of the response.

The ratification of the North Atlantic Pact in 1949 inaugurated a new emphasis on regional security and a corresponding diminution of faith in the concept of collective security on a universal basis. More fundamentally, NATO and succeeding regional agencies became increasingly important instruments to promote the American policy of containing the expansion of Soviet power.

The establishment of the Rio Treaty for mutual security in the event of aggression in the Western Hemisphere was also to be linked with the other regional systems though the Communist threat was not as immediate. The Act of Chapultepec of 1945 had preceded the rift between the United States and the Soviet Union and prepared the hemisphere for a formal security pact that was signed in Rio de Janeiro in 1947. It embodied as strong a mutual security commitment as the North Atlantic Pact in providing under Article 3 "that an armed attack by any State against an American state shall be considered as an attack against all the American States." With the signing of the Bogota Charter in 1948, the Rio Pact became the military cornerstone of the inter-American system formalized as the Organization of American States and an expression of the containment policy as applied to the Western Hemisphere.

The North Atlantic Treaty Organization was justified as a legitimate exercise of the right of collective self-defense as provided under Article

51 of the Charter. Article 7 declared: "This treaty does not affect, and shall not be interpreted as affecting, in any way the rights and obligations under the Charter of the parties which are members of the United Nations, or the primary responsibility of the Security Council for the maintenance of international peace and security."

This deliberate effort to harmonize the spirit of NATO with the wider obligations of the United Nations concealed, however, an obvious disillusionment with the capacity of the universal organization to ensure peace as revealed in the remarks of three of the official signers of the Pact: (Dirk Stikker, foreign minister of the Netherlands) "The treaty we are about to sign marks the end of an illusion: the hope that the United Nations would, by itself, ensure international peace;" (Paul Henri-Spaak of Belgium) "Those who today are angered or saddened because the principles of universal collective security contemplated by the United Nations Charter are to be supplemented by a system more restricted—will find some subjects for reflection;" and (Lester Pearson of Canada) "The North Atlantic Treaty was born out of fear and frustration . . ." [5]

In connection with the creation of NATO, Professor Ross Berkes makes the following penetrating comment:[6] "The evidence of deliberate harmonization of NATO with the United Nations would make it easy, in one sense, to conclude by affirming a spiritual bond of affinity and mutuality. One cannot contest, however, the recognition that NATO symbolizes the division of the world into hostile and tension-ridden power blocs: a situation not conducive to the operation of a universal organization based upon fundamental agreement of basic principles. This situation is not compatible with a system of genuine collective security."

Shortly after the ratification of the North Atlantic Pact the attention of the West became focused on the Far East. With the outbreak of the Korean conflict in 1950 and the triumph of the Communist revolution in China in 1949, the United States was alerted to the vulnerability of Western defenses in Asia. Despite the success of the limited collective security action in Korea by the United Nations that halted the Communist drive for hegemony in the Far East, it was recognized that only the fortuitous absence of the Soviet delegate from the Security Council permitted United Nations action in that conflict. Though the United States-sponsored Uniting for Peace Resolution introduced into the General Assembly in 1950 attempted to fill in the void in the Council by elevating the Assembly to a more prominent role in peace enforcement, the need for stronger guarantees to resist future aggression in the Far East was recognized.

Immediately precipitated by the defeat of the French in Indo-China in 1954, a series of multilateral conferences among the United States, its European allies, and three friendly nations of Southeast Asia culminated in the signing of the Manila Treaty in 1954 that created the Southeast Asia Treaty Organization.[7]

In contrast with NATO, the Asian defense agency reflects a weaker collective security commitment since an attack upon one signatory is not considered as an attack on all; it involves only the obligation for mutual consultation. This may be explained by the greater political and economic diversity of the member states than exists within NATO, as well as by the fact that the majority of members are external to the geographic area defined in the treaty and would therefore be less likely to consider an attack on an Asian member a threat to their vital interests. The contrasting environments of the regional defense systems of Western Europe and Southeast Asia have been noted: [8] "In Europe the problem was to strengthen and organize a group of nations which (with certain minor exceptions) are geographically contiguous, and (again with certain exceptions) possessed large and diversified . . . industrial economies. (In Asia the) . . . countries were widely separated geographically . . . [and] those located upon the mainland were, without exception, traditionalist societies, and with little modern industry and low military capabilities."

A survey of the nature of the circumstances which prompted the establishment of Western regional systems would be incomplete without mention of the efforts to create a barrier against Soviet expansion in the Middle East. Efforts to develop a regional security system there were complicated by the Arab League. Established in part to eliminate Western influence from the region, the Arab states maintained an intense hostility toward the West whom they blamed for the creation of Israel. The anti-colonial character of the League militated against efforts by the United States to induce the members of that agency to join in a Middle East Defense Organization. With the demise of that plan search for an alternative organization to deter Soviet ambitions in the region culminated in the Baghdad Pact.

The Baghdad Pact began as a bilateral agreement between Turkey and Iraq and widened into a multilateral alliance with the accession of Great Britain, Pakistan, and Iran in 1955 to form "the

'northern tier' defense system against the Soviet Union." [9] It provided for mutual cooperation for defense in accordance with Article
51 of the United Nations Charter, but contained no firm obligations
except mutual consultation through a permanent, council, secretariat,
and various committees. A formidable gap arose in 1958 with the
overthrow of the Hashemite monarch of Iraq and the subsequent
secession of that state from the arrangement, thereby exposing a
crucial vulnerability of the "northern tier" to Soviet influence. Re-
christening of the arrangement in 1959 as CENTO (Central Treaty
Organization) failed to produce any appreciable degree of political
or military integration, and the attractiveness of the agency for
Turkey, Pakistan, and Iran is in danger of being undermined by
the refusal of the United States to participate as a permanent member
and to assign permanent military forces to the region. [10]

While emphasis has been placed upon the development of Western
security arrangements to fill in the vacuum created by the decline of
the United Nations as a peace-enforcing agency, centrifugal tendencies
toward regionalism have involved the Communist bloc as well. The
Soviet Union has also sought security in more limited associations
than the United Nations. Although it is a moot legal question
as to whether regionalism in the Communist sphere partakes of the
characteristics common to orthodox regional groupings (that is, a
multilateral cooperation among independent and sovereign nations),
there can be no doubt as to the reality of the Warsaw Pact organization which superseded the earlier series of bilateral treaties concluded between the Soviet Union and its East European satellites. [11]

Depending less on formal treaties than on the ideological fervor
of the Marxist-Leninist doctrine, Soviet military occupation, and a
pronounced degree of East European economic dependence on the
Soviet Union, "the effective military coordination of Eastern European forces and policies with those of Moscow was so complete as
to have resulted in common tables of organization (and) standardized
armaments and uniforms." [12]

Professor Ernst Haas has analyzed the rationale of the Warsaw
Pact in terms of a countervailing response of the Communist world
to NATO and especially to German participation in NATO through
its membership in the Western European Union. [13] "The Pact coin-
cided with a strong offensive to undermine the will of the NATO
partners to continue the allance. It was, in effect, a negotiating device
to induce the West to withdraw from Germany or to limit NATO

commitments without making any real reciprocal concession." An additional incentive may have been the desire to give a semblance of national equality to the satellites by developing a multilateral framework instead of continuing the bilateral network of treaty relations that gave the appearance of Soviet domination. [14]

The preceding survey of the growth of regional security organizations since 1945 reveals that the immediate impetus for the launching of these agences was the early disintegration of the United Nations as guarantor of international peace and security brought about by the failure of the United States and the Soviet Union to establish the necessary harmony to sustain the organization.

It reflected the emergence of two rival conceptions of world order: a liberal democratic conception of a universal order of independent and sovereign units managed by the major powers and a Soviet conception of a universal order of rival ideological systems preliminary to the emergence of a historically inevitable Communist world order.

From regional security agencies we turn now to an examination of the growth of non-military regional groups since 1945. Though the separation of military and non-military regional systems is difficult to justify because military groups are affected by the economic and social policies of member states, it is convenient to distinguish these organizations from those agencies whose primary purpose is economic and social development rather than defense.

The emergence of regional economic and social cooperation may be viewed as an outgrowth of the gradual obsolescence of the nation-state as a self-sufficient economic and social entity. [15] In Western Europe, where such cooperation has proceeded furthest, movement away from exclusive reliance on the nation-state is progressing and may culminate in a regional federation or confederation. Arising out of a complex of political, military and economic considerations, Western European unification is also being imitated in the non-Western areas. We will first examine the evolution of regionalism in Western Europe and then comment critically on the possibilities for duplicating regional cooperation in the less developed areas.

Western Europe As a Case Study in Regional Integration. While the term integration is subject to a variety of meanings and interpretations, it is impossible to proceed without a general indication of the nature of the concept. In simplest language and in the European context, it has been described as "the merging of interests and the entering upon systematic cooperation between governments on a permanent basis." [16] In practice the process of integration may be manifested by the growth of military, political, and economic ties among nation-states.

As in the case of the various regional security agencies, it has also been customary to attribute the growth of regional economic and social integration in Western Europe as a reaction to the threat of Soviet imperialism. To the extent that economic and social unification enhanced European military security such an assumption has validity. On the other hand regional economic and social integration may be an end in itself as well as a means toward the attainment of greater military power to offset an external threat.

Circumstances within nation-states must also be considered in addition to external conditions in attempting to understand the dynamics of regional integration. What are these circumstances with regard to Western Europe and what do they reveal regarding the adequacy of the nation-state to satisfy the rapidly changing needs and demands of its citizens?

Part of the answer may lie in the "decline of the territorial state" as a result of complex changes that have created a situation in Western Europe, and the rest of the world for that matter, where nations can no longer function effectively as self-contained military, economic, or political units but must seek wider cooperation to solve common problems. In Western Europe military integration was necessary to deter Soviet aggression; political integration to restore the continent to its former eminence in world affairs and to reinforce economic and military cooperation; and economic integration to free Europe from economic dependence upon the United States. [17]

Western European regionalism was hastened by internal economic and political factors as well as by the more obvious external threat to the region. [18] Leading European statesmen urged unification as a pragmatic solution to the problem of maximizing European economic and political potential in a world in which political and economic power seemed to be inexorably and permanently gravitating to the United States and the Soviet Union. Underlying their views was a certain disillusionment with the excessive nationalism of the past.

In addition to the above factors that have influenced the six-nation core of "Inner Europe," integration within that area has also been faciltated by the absence of any severe disparity in power among the participating countries. France and West Germany appear to dominate "Little Europe" but neither power has been able to dictate unilaterally the future course of integration. At the same time, the regional grouping of "Little Europe" is not saddled with the customary weakness of small-state regional groups that have depended upon extra-regional support in order to sustain their viability.

Insofar as the process of European economic and social integration in "Little Europe" is concerned, Professor Ernst Haas in his important study *The Uniting of Europe* has provided valuable insights into the complex interaction of private groups, political parties, public opinion, and government action involved in the establishment of the European Coal and Steel Community and as a stimulus to further integration during the period 1950-57. Though his conclusions are limited to six nations of Western Europe, they may furnish useful hypotheses to be applied in connection with economic and social unification in the non-Western areas.

Professor Haas discovered that the process of building regional communities consists of a clear differentiation of three factors: background conditions, political process, and consequent conditions. Among the crucial background factors related to economic integration in Western Europe are the ideologies, attitudes, and expectations of the organized major governmental and non-governmental groups. A general identity of aims regarding the desirability of unification existed among these groups but for different reasons. For some unity was necessary to overcome the political and economic weakness caused by the war with its overdependence on the United States while other groups ". . . equated a United Europe with a general economic, social and cultural regeneration, achieving a new synthesis beyond the old issues of national hatreds, wars and class conflict." [18]

Fragmentation of opinion regarding economic integration "facilitated the eventual establishment of close links on a regional basis of communication among ideologically allied political and economic elites." [19] However, the growth of regional communications for the most part occurred after the establishment of the ECSC. This supports the commonly held assumption that successful political institutions promote community consciousness which in turn strengthens the institutions and expands their functions.

Subsequent to the establishment of the ECSC, Haas found that [20] "a closer rapport among trade unions, trade associations, political parties, and senior civil servants began to develop, a process which eventually 'spilled over' from the realm of coal and steel to the field of general economic unification—or the Common Market—and acquired an independent momentum perhaps in 1955."

In confirming the view that the sector approach to economic integration is inadequate, Haas called attention to the impossibility of isolating a basic industrial complex (coal and steel) from the other sectors of the economy since problems are created that can only be solved by further integration: [21] "once governments have committed themselves . . . to certain common measures . . . they can resolve future problems of implementing the agreement only by further delegation of power to the center [for] . . . withdrawal would imply a sacrifice of economic advantage—a step not taken lightly by elected politicians." Economic integration therefore is not solely conditioned by the appearance of an external threat to regional security but is also a function of internal needs and demands.

Demand for increasing regional activity is not based on theoretical principles but on essentially practical motivations in which regional integration serves to secure increasing economic prosperity and well-being. Haas concluded that while there are no completely common background factors in Western Europe a number of basic environmental factors contributed to integration: [22]

• A common pluralistic social structure except for Greece, Turkey, Portugal, and parts of Spain and southern Italy. Various well-organized socio-economic groups compete for political power and social status by mobilizing the masses in trade unions, trade associations, and political parties.

• A very high degree of economic development even in those states whose major products are agricultural (high productivity, consumption, and investment). Industralization is correlated with urbanization and with growing demands for government service and with greater dependence on foreign or regional trade.

• Ideological patterns of homogeneity among political parties observable in Scandinavia and among Europe of the Six except for anti-parliamentary minorities in France and Italy.

• Fear of a common enemy is a precondition for military integration, but the common enemy may be a more subtle manifestation such as the fear of external groupings of culturally and economically suspect forces: these considerations were not irrelevant to the "third force" argument articulated by various groups within "little Europe."

• While external factors may produce tendencies toward unity, they are never sufficient in themselves as explanations for the rate and intensity of the process of regional integration.

On the basis of the above conclusions, variance in the growth of political community may be observed through comparison of the European Common Market and the Council of Europe. Integration in the larger Council of Europe has been inhibited by the admixture of pluralistic and nonpluralistic social structures whereas the homogeneity of ideology, economy, and social structure in the smaller area of "Little Europe" facilitated the expansion of transnational cooperation.

Summarizing the lessons of his study of European integration, Professor Haas asserts that [23] "environmentally, integration fares best in situations representing the rational interests of urban-industrial society, groups seeking to maximize their economic benefits and dividing along regionally homogenous ideological-political lines. Changing national policy inhibits integration unless compensated by strong central institutions maximizing the spill-over process."

Although it is not the purpose of this study to analyze the process of economic and social integration, it is appropriate to develop a few generalizations based in part on the investigation of Professor Haas. In the absence of substantial empirical research in the field of regional integration, the following hypotheses are suggested as working assumptions for future research:

• Expanding regional organization presupposes an underlying community solidarity reflecting a certain similarity of economic, political, and social systems.

• Regional integration is an interrelated process affecting several functional sectors characterized by an increasing willingness among participant states to relinquish exclusive control and jurisdiction over military, economic, and social policy.

• Multifunctionalism tends to increase regional integration whereas single-purpose or single-function organization retards it.

• The ultimate end of a process of economic and social unification successfully under way is the establishment of a regional political community transcending formerly separate and autonomous units. It may be federative or confederative.

• Western Europe, or at least Europe of the Six, appears to be in the incipient stages of a movement away from exclusive reliance upon the nation-state which may culminate in the creation of a genuine regional political community.

• The success of Western European regionalism is reflected not only by an underlying degree of economic and social solidarity as expressed in compatible ideological, industrial, and sociological forms of organization but to the absence of any striking power disparity among the member states.

• The experience of European integration is not automatically transferable to the non-Western regions because of fundamental dissimilarities in the internal environments.

We will now attempt to verify these working hypotheses. That a modicum of community solidarity is prerequisite for regional cooperation has long been accepted by scholars of regionalism. In Western Europe an underlying cultural unity may be traced to the Holy Roman Empire, the Renaissance, and the Age of the Enlightenment. Despite the existence of separate national cultural traditions, the nations of Western Europe were the fountainhead for the enduring aesthetic, intellectual, and cultural values associated with modern Western civilization. It was here that the first plans for a united European community were developed centuries ago in order to take advantage of the common fabric of civilization that permeates the continent. The existence of common religious traditions of Christianity to some extent has been responsible for restraining excesses of war and conflict and in uniting the peoples of Western Europe in a common spiritual framework.

Though the geographic concentration of many nations into a relatively compact area has not always produced stability and order, the proximity between and among the individual nations created a growing awareness of political, economic, and cultural interdependence especially after the Industrial Revolution spurred improvements in transportation and communications and the expansion of international trade. When this increasing interdependence was interrupted by two cataclysmic world wars of the twentieth century, the leading European statesmen keenly recognized the need for a new solidarity to replace the excessive nationalism that had reduced the political, economic, and cultural prestige of Europe through devastation of her material and moral resources. The growth of a new regional internationalism since 1945 is in part a reaction to the excessive fragmentation of the past in an effort to self-preserve the future.

Finally, Western Europe has long possessed a natural economic unity whose full potential was stifled by the existence of artificial barriers to the free exchange of goods and services and the movement of labor. The recent abandonment of these long standing impediments to economic growth and efficiency through creation of the European Economic Community has resulted in sizeable increases in international trade among the six nations whose complementary economies constitute a natural and now expanded economic market. Economic integration has been facilitated by a close interdependence in which "the countries were connected by a dense network of low-cost transportation and communications, and there was a high degree of specialization, based on intra-European trade"; [25] integration thus served "to consolidate and intensify an already substantial degree of interdependence." [26]

Community consciousness and tangible geographic and economic interests do not necessarily produce regional integration. Various common interests of Western Europe existed for centuries but only recently have they been merged in an evolving economic and social cooperation. This leads to the observation that the existence of shared values, traditions, and tangible interests may be a necessary but not a sufficient condition for international integration. When combined with the appearance of an external economic or military threat and declining national economic and political power, a fertile basis emerges for the launching of institutional cooperation. The absence of such unifying characteristics in the underdeveloped areas coupled with an intense nationalism impedes regional integration among the non-Western nations.

In connection with the process of regional integration, the second hypothesis postulates that the process of developing and furthering common interests is reflected in several sectors simultaneously rather in one sector or function.

Professor Haas, however, believes that the history of European integration points to the autonomy rather the interdependence of functional contexts, asserting that "integrative forces which flow from one kind of activity do not necessarily infect other activities, even if carried out by the same organization." Although it would be difficult to prove that NATO led to the ECSC which in turn prompted the ill-fated European Political Community, these three functional sectors were closely interwoven in the evolution of regional cooperation. Integrative forces in one sector may not permeate another sector but on the other hand interacting influences and pressures may be generated.

It could be argued that in the period following the establishment

of NATO, plans for a closer unity developed among the continental
European states reflected in the economic federalism of the European
Coal and Steel Community. The successful beginning of the ECSC
in turn encouraged the six member nations to apply the federative
approach to the military sector. The European Army plan (European
Defense Community) was in part a reaction to the loosely integrated
NATO system which was largely a paper organization in 1950. It
was also realized that the coordination of the military and economic
communities required a political institution for guidance. In fact
Article 38 of the Defense Community Treaty directed the combined
assemblies of the two functional communities to investigate the
creation to investigate the creation of a "permanent organization . . .
[of] federal or confederal structure" These investigations culminated
in the Statute of the European Political Community.

Despite the collapse of this trilateral scheme in 1954 when the
EDC treaty failed to be ratified by France, the close connection
between military, economic, and political unification planning if
not achievement would seem to indicate that functional contexts are
not autonomous but interdependent. In fact Professor Haas appears
to confirm this hypothesis: [27] "demands and expectations for further
integrating measures are voiced as a result of performance in previously federated spheres of governmental activity. Performance is
held inadequate because of an insufficient grant of powers or timid
policy on the part of central authorities: hence the claim for new
federal powers to achieve better performance is a direct outgrowth
of the earlier institutional system and the realignment of group
expectations produced through it . . ."

In discussing the interrelatedness of the integration process in
Western Europe, a recent study concludes that [28] "the integration
of economic interests is hardly possible without some degree of social
integration. Even when economic integration is given priority, as
is the case with the more effective of the European institutions . . .
some degree of political integration also takes place. On the other
hand, peaceful political integration can be realized only if and when
economic, social, and cultural interests have reached a high measure
of solidarity."

Thus the key to the process of regional integration in highly literate
and industrialized societies is the interdependence of economic, political, and military sectors, making it difficult to integrate one sector
without at least attempting unification in the others. The more

difficult problem of the ideal sequence for integration would seem to depend upon the appropriateness for unification of the military, economic, and political spheres. If the sequence in Western Europe has followed in this fashion, it may be as a result of the influence of an external military threat prompting military integration which in turn required for its effectiveness economic integration that generated momentum for a genuine political community to coordinate the process of unification.

A third hypothesis is intimately related to the preceding premise. It is based on the model of inter-nation relations discussed in Chapter II which predicted that when a number of important needs exist simultaneously within a number of national publics multifunctional collaboration results; where functional cooperation is limited to one sphere the process of integration is likely to be retarded when the need which precipitated the cooperation has been satisfied. [29]

Examination of the process of European integration tends to support this hypothesis. The background conditions which fostered unification included not only an underlying geographic, economic, and cultural solidarity but internal political, economic, and cultural weakness induced by the cumulative effect of two world wars that had greatly reduced the prestige of the continent. In the international system national power had gravitated for the first time in history to non-European states—the United States and the Soviet Union. Additionally, the external threat posed by the threat of Soviet takeover in combination with the internal factors provoked needs and demands for security that could not be satisfied by military rejuvenation alone but required a concomitant political and economic regeneration. The coexistence of military, economic, and political needs that could not be fulfilled nationally led to multifunctional regional collaboration. The fact that progress in each of these sectors has been uneven and fluctuating does not refute the essential hypothesis.

We may also observe that where military cooperation exists as a single function perspective as in NATO, there is a tendency for the urgency of cooperation to recede wherever the member states perceive that the external threat of hostility has abated. Although threat abatement has been spasmodic since the inception of NATO, there appears to be a lessening of internal solidarity whenever it appears to the European members that the Soviet Union relaxes its bellicose attitude toward the West.

A fourth hypothesis is that the ultimate end of a process of unification successfully under way is the establishment of a political community transcending formerly autonomous nation-states in a federative or confederative structure. Political integration has been defined as [30] "the process whereby political actors in several distinct national settings are persuaded to shift their loyalties, expectations, and political activities toward a new and larger center, whose institutions possess or demand jurisdiction over the pre-existing national states.'"

Again we may substantiate this hypothesis by empirical observation. The gradual consolidation of common interests in Western Europe developed first in the military sphere under NATO and "spilled over" into the narrow functionalism of a coal and steel community out of which more ambitious economic integration has emerged in the European Common Market. The continued success of these organs involves something more than the technical problems of specialized functional cooperation. The ECSC was as much a device for bringing France and Germany into political harmony as an economic venture while the European Common Market may be viewed as a foundation upon which a later political union could be erected. [31]

No more convincing proof of the political nature of the Common Market exists than the following comments of the President of its Executive Commission, Dr. Walter Hallstein, delivered before the Parliamentary Assembly of the three functional communities in March, 1958: [32]

". . . our Community is a supranational institution with its own political personality. That is shown not only by the fact that the federal organ, consisting of members of the six Governments and known as the Council, is largely governed by the majority principle, so that there can be no veto by individual Governments. Nor is it determined by the mere fact that this Community has its own purely supranational Executive, namely our Commission, whose members are subject to no instructions of any kind from national authorities, nor indeed by the mere fact that there is a Court of Justice which, in a way—binding upon all—the six States and their citizens alike—is responsible for protecting the Treaty rules and regulations against infringement. Proof that our Community represents a new outstanding achievement . . . lies above all in the existence of this august Assembly and the role it is intended to fulfill, as the organ which gives free and completely independent expression to the will of the six-nation Community. . . ."

Whether the Assembly expresses a supranational character is unclear, however. Its powers are strictly advisory and recommendatory. If it provides a forum for the discussion of community economic and social policy, its delegates are not yet free from the tinge of national interests since they are appointed by their own national parliaments though the EEC treaty envisions the time when they will be directly elected by the people of the community.

More fundamentally, the problem of achieving European economic and social integration cannot be separated from the problem of attaining political integration. The relationship is reciprocal in the sense that the success of regional agencies depends to a large degree on the extent to which the countries represented maintain political solidarity in the future. Conversely, these experiments in multi-national cooperation reflect a growing sense of community of interests among the six nations without which political unification would be impossible.

Although the initial pattern of integration began in non-political sectors, it is also possible that regional unification may begin politically and then fan out into military and economic integration as in the case of the consolidation of the American colonies into a federal system. Within Western Europe, however, this has not been the pattern.

The history of Western European regionalism reveals a progressive expansion of centralized decision-making bodies exercising jurisdiction over the six nations of "Little Europe" with a rapid increase in the growth of various tasks allotted to regional institutions. On the basis of this pattern observable in economic and social sectors, it appears that continental Europe of the Six is in the incipient stages of a movement away from exclusive reliance on the nation-state which may culminate in the attainment of regional political community. Possibilities for a wider geographic integration embracing Britain and the Scandinavia are contingent on whether or not Great Britain succeeds in entering the European Common Market and pulling the other members of the European Free Trade Association into that organization.

An important subsidiary question is the extent to which the new regional institutions of the Six are in fact genuine departures from national sovereignty in the sectors they purport to regulate. The European Coal and Steel Community was a deliberate departure from the traditional intergovernmental pattern of European cooperation. A High Authority was empowered to issue legally binding rules covering

a six-nation area coal and steel sector without regard for the jurisdiction of any one unit but for the region as a whole. These decisions
could be taken by majority vote and the members of the High
Authority were technical experts rather than politicians. While there
is still disagreement as to the independence of the High Authority
from the more politically motivated Council of Ministers, the recommendations of the expert body have in most instances been accepted
without complaint from the member governments. [33]

In a well known study of the ECSC, Professor William Diebold concluded that the community is a mixed system of nationalism and
supranationalism: [34] "the issue of national vs. supranational power
is a real one, but it is not the only issue; it could become crucial, but
during the transitional period it has not been dominant. The main
question has been how the governments and the High Authority
could work out methods of combining their forces to produce a sensible
governance of the Community economy, to promote the common
market. . . . [However] the substance and consequences of the actions are considerably more important than their form. The High
Authority's policy of seeking a broad area of agreement . . . greatly
helped in this process. The basic fact is that the governments have
political responsibility of a sort the High Authority escapes. This
establishes limits to what can be done that may not correspond to
the legal dispositions of the Treaty. In law and in political fact the
Community is a mixed system. The continuing importance of governmental action is clear, but the supranational power is also real."

If the experiment in supranationalism in coal and steel has not
resulted in a marked degree of enthusiasm for this pattern of interstate
cooperation, the legal and constitutional structures of the European
Economic Community and the European Atomic Energy Community
possess traces of power transcending national states without their
unanimous consent. [35] Moreover, the conjointment of the three functional communities in a common legislative assembly reflects the
desire by the six nations of "Little Europe" to coordinate and plan
future integration on the basis of an emerging regional solidarity
even though this organ is without binding powers.

In addition, the three functional communities now have executive
organs composed of experts "vested with limited but real 'supranational' powers . . . and may initiate proposals and make decisions
on a variety of matters laid down in the respective treaties." [36] Whether
this expanding economic integration culminates in the establishment

of a regional federation or confederation is uncertain especially as a result of the divisive influences introduced by French veto of British entry into the EEC in January, 1963. The acceleration of European unity will also be affected by the intensity of the Soviet threat as well as by the necessity for overcoming vestiges of national separatism.

Our sixth hypothesis stipulated that the success of Western European regionalism is conditioned not only by favorable background factors such as an underlying economic and social solidarity expressed in similar forms of industrialism and a pluralistic social structure but may also be attributed to the absence of any striking power disparity among the member states. There are of course differentials of power as France and West Germany are stronger individually than any of the other four member states. Yet neither has been able to convert the region into a "sphere of influence" under its own hegemony and set in motion the resentments and antagonisms endemic to great power domination of lesser powers. There is also some doubt as to whether a Franco-West German axis, as has been suggested by some commentators, will be able to dictate the future evolution of "Little Europe." Clear evidence of the resistance of the smaller states to acquiesce in General DeGaulle's attempt to exert French hegemonic influence is their refusal to accept suggestions for political union until the problem of Britain's entry into the European Common Market has been resolved.

Similarly, the coexistence of large and small powers within "Little Europe" has brought about an association which is singularly free from the weaknesses that plague small state regional groupings since the region has become independent of external economic support. If it is objected that the six nations are still reliant upon the United States for military security, they are becoming more and more desirous of developing an independent nuclear deterrent system.

A final hypothesis is that the experience of European integration is not automatically transferable to the underdeveloped areas because of fundamental dissimilarities in the economic, political, and social environments between the two contexts. [37] This hypothesis rests in part on the findings of Professor Haas relating to the success of the European integration: industrialized economies of a high degree of specialization; pluralistic social structures in which key elites and the masses are mobilized for political action; and ideologically homogenous political systems. All of these favorable background factors are missing or only beginning to be developed in the less developed regions.

Regional unification in the non-Western areas must await a greater political maturity and stability among the states located there. In many areas intra-regional rivalries act as divisive forces as nationalism functions as a deterrent to wider unity. While regional cooperation is being advanced through common market arrangements in Latin America and Africa, such arrangements rely on a much less favorable set of economic circumstances than exist in Western Europe. In the underdeveloped areas "the foreign trade . . . consists essentially of exchanging primary products for manufactured goods from the advanced industrial countries. The trade routes and internal transportation systems are oriented towards the ports for trade with Europe and North America." [38] To the extent that these countries become industrialized the trade pattern may be reversed, but the discouraging reality is that such economic modernization and specialization is only in its infancy in most of these nations. A more detailed analysis of the possibilities for regional integration in the non-Western areas follows.

Regional Integration in the Non-Western Areas. In exploring the basis for regionalism in Latin America, the Middle East, and Asia, Professor Haas raises an important question: [39] European integration reveals the importance of institutional forces in accelerating further unity, but what factors account for the lack of acceleration provided by oas bodies, seato meetings, and Arab League conferences? The non-Western setting of these groups may provide some clues as to the role of cultural differences in fostering or retarding integration.

A thorough examination of the political processes of these regional agencies would be required in order to find the answers to these and other questions. In the absence of such research, however, it may be desirable to approach the problem of why political institutions have failed to accelerate integration in the non-Western areas from the perspective of the various theories of regionalism explored in an earlier stage of this study.

These theories reveal that regional communities are affected by both internal factors of cultural, political, and economic environment as well as by the wider dynamics of international politics. Expansion of solidarity may be enhanced by policies of defense but unless this can be broadened into nonmilitary avenues of collaboration there is apt to be a relaxation of solidarity proportional with the decrease in the external threat or indeed its disappearance.

Throughout the non-Western areas therefore a major retarding factor in the acceleration of regional economic and social cooperation may lie in the inadequacy of regional institutions of the Arab League, SEATO, and CENTO to develop or diversify their original narrow basis of defense into broader and more positive channels. In turn this failure may be based not so much on the institutions as such as on the inability of the member states to cooperate except with regard to the most tangible threat to their independence. As we have previously indicated, moreover, such cooperation may also be hampered by the existence of economies that are more competitive than complementary.

In all of the underdeveloped regions despite common cultural, religious, or historical traditions and the similarity of economic and social aspirations, there are countervailing and frequently disintegrative forces that have impeded any meaningful regional integration. Of all of these forces extreme nationalism is perhaps the most significant. If regional integration of national communities is the product of a reinforcing and progressive interaction between national governments and regional institutions in which the former are gradually absorbed into the latter, then it would appear that the contemporary tendency of many of these nations to consider the needs of their own national committees first rather than those of a regional community is not conducive to regional unity.

A recent report from the Center of International Affairs at Harvard analyzing the impact of ideology on the underdeveloped states came to these important conclusions: [40]

(1) "On the basis of . . . postwar experience . . . progress [toward integration] seems to be least difficult to achieve when the nations involved are what one could call mature nations: i.e. countries which have existed as nations for a long period, in the sense of having been independent long enough to appreciate the blessings and pitfalls of independence.

(2) "Even when optimum conditions exist, progress in the establishment of transnational bonds finds its limits in the indifference of the masses to regional organization and the tendency of most citizens to identify their destinies with the nation rather than with a larger grouping."

If these conclusions are applied to the non-Western areas, the prospects are not encouraging. The majority of these nations are so preoccupied with the establishment of their own national identities that they are unfavorably disposed to seek wider cooperation unless they perceive tangible rewards quickly. As we have indicated, the possibilities of such rewards coming quickly through regional economic groupings are not bright. Secondly, if we accept Professor Haas' conclusions regarding the crucial role of mass support in promoting regional integration, enthusiasm within the non-Western regions for cooperation is confined largely to only a narrow minority of the population with the masses both unable and probably unwilling to comprehend the advantages of wider cooperation.

It is not to be expected therefore that regionalism will proceed at the same pace which has developed in Western Europe. In addition to the aforementioned difficulties, there are varying degrees of political instability emanating not only from the post-independence problem of maintaining law and order but also from the lack of adequately trained civil servants, marked gaps in standards of living between the elites and the masses, rising population pressures that threaten to retard the most ambitious economic development programs, and wide variations in the political and economic levels within the regions themselves. Before regional cooperation can become effective, these problems will have to be solved or at least a start must be made toward their improvement. Finally, since regionalism presupposes a willingness to modify nationalism with internationalism, important changes in the attitude of most of these states will be required. Many are caught up in such a wave of rising expectations for their peoples that nationalism rather than internationalism is apt to be the dominant force in the decades immediately ahead. All of these factors lead to the conclusion that while regional cooperation for economic and social development is feasible in the non-Western areas, the pace will be much slower than in Western Europe.

CHAPTER VI

REGIONALISM AND THE UNITED NATIONS

In the previous chapter the reasons for the growth of regional organizations since 1945 and the various components of the process of integration in Western Europe were analyzed. This chapter will assess the contemporary political and economic relationships between these organizations and the United Nations.

The dynamics of universalism and regionalism will be approached in terms of the two most commonly cited functions of international organization: security and welfare. To what extent have regional security agencies succeeded as substitutes for a deteriorating universal order? What may we conclude regarding the alleged superiority of regional agencies in the peaceful settlement of international disputes? Insofar as regional welfare agencies are concerned, what has been the degree of their effectiveness and to what extent have they conflicted with the economic and social operations of the United Nations? Are there any possibilities for developing coordinating links between the United Nations and regional security and welfare agencies?

Regional Security and the United Nations. As analyzed earlier the compromise between universalism and regionalism prescribed in the United Nations Charter has been eroded by the establishment of numerous regional agencies functioning outside the control and supervision of the universal organization.[1] Prior to the emergence of the disequilibrium between global and regional forms of cooperation, the United Nations undertook to adjust itself to an environment of great-power conflict alien to the concept of world order formulated at the San Francisco Conference. Under the leadership of the United States, the General Assembly in November, 1950 passed the famous Uniting for Peace Resolution in order to prevent the Soviet Union from using the veto to frustrate the prosecution of United Nations enforcement action in Korea. In a more fundamental sense the resolution was designed to permit the United Nations to survive as an enforcement agency for collective security by assigning the General Assembly peace-keeping responsibilities in those situations in which the Security Council was inactivated by great power conflict.

Empowering the Assembly to discuss situations threatening the peace and to recommend to its members appropriate measures for the maintenance of peace and security, the resolution was noteworthy with regard to the role it envisioned for regional security agencies. A Collective Measures Committee was established to investigate the possibility of using regional agencies as adjuncts for the maintenance of peace and security. No action, however, has been taken by regional agencies to place forces at the disposal of the General Assembly as recommended by the Committee. Though the resolution may have resuscitated the rapidly disintegrating peace machinery of the United Nations by revitalizing the principle of collective security, the Collective Measures Committee has been unable to reintegrate regional security agencies into the framework of the United Nations. The disequilibrium between universalism and regionalism therefore was not reversed by the Uniting for Peace Resolution.

If the United Nations has been incapacitated as the dominant agency for peace enforcement because of the unexpected schism among the great powers, what about the performances of the various regional security agencies as instrumentalities for the preservation or attainment of world order? These will now be examined in some detail with regard to their military efficacy as well as their record as peaceful settlement mechanisms.

As stated in the introduction to this study, the author is fully aware of the fact that the numerous regional security agencies created since 1945 are inadequate embodiments of the theoretical prerequisites of a universal collective security system. Despite the prevailing tendency of statesmen and politicians to identify such agencies as instruments of collective security, they are in reality reflections of the inability of the international community to organize itself effectively for enforcement action on a universal basis. The various regional security agencies are selective rather than collective security mechanisms: they aim to bring about security from aggression for only restricted or limited groupings of states; the ideal of impartial action implicit in the Wilsonian concept of universal collective security is missing for the aggressor is known in advance; and in certain regional security systems the obligation to come to the assistance of a beleaguered state is not unconditional but conditioned by the approval of the duly constituted national decision-making authorities.

In many respects multilateral and bilateral security treaties of the United States and the Soviet Union mark a return to the pre-World

War I period of competing alliances which Woodrow Wilson believed to be a major cause of war and conflict. Proclaimed as strictly defensive arrangements in conformity with the principles of the United Nations Charter, these alliances are considered offensive and hostile groupings by the state to which they are directed. In this sense their formation contributes to the tension and insecurity they were designed to replace. Moreover, regional security agencies not only heighten tensions between the superpowers but also affect and are affected by the third major grouping of states, the uncommitted or nonaligned nations.[2] As neutrals in the cold war, these nations are similar to the traditional neutrals of Switzerland, Belgium, and Sweden by their refusal to add power to rival blocs, but dissimilar in that "positive" neutralists have "engaged in an active policy of play-off and unsolicited mediation between the great powers."[3]

The neutralists of the modern era have refused to participate in either of the major power blocs because of the conviction that such blocs exacerbate international tensions and increase the danger of war. Preferring maximum maneuverability in order to take advantage of their strategic positions they also view membership in military pacts as restrictions on their newly won independence. Nonaligned nations believe that they may be effective as mediators between the United States and the Soviet Union.

In addition neutralists have been critical of military alliances on the basis of the nature of contemporary international relations. Not only does membership in such groupings reduce national freedom of maneuver in foreign affairs, it also entails great risks since alignment with nuclear powers increases the danger of national survival in the event of nuclear war. Nonalignment therefore is viewed as a means of escaping nuclear destruction though the chances for such immunity in the event of total war are questionable.

Another criticism is that affiliation with former colonial powers is a kind of neo-colonialism in which the small power is subjected to a renewal of Western influence and control. Alliances not only create problems for small states who succumb to the blandishments of great powers, they also may affect the status of those powers within the same region that eschew alignment. Professor Liska has observed the deleterious impact of Western alliances in non-Western areas: [4]

"In the eyes of Nasser and his followers the Baghdad Pact disrupted the common front of the Arab League against Israel and, under the guise of an anti-Soviet front, intensified the ambitions of the Iraqi

elite with regard to Syria and Egypt; from Nehru's viewpoint SEATO
has enabled Pakistan to be tougher towards India and Afghanistan,
and Thailand to press its ambitions against Cambodia.   The affected
states cannot but react by giving a militant slant to their non-align-
ment, so as to enhance their nuisance value, penalize the great power
ally of their adversary, and secure countervailing outside assistance.
By introducing arms and discord into the region, the alliance of a
small state with a great power constitutes in Nehru's words a 'reversal
of the process of liberation.' "

On the other hand, neutralism has introduced some restraints on the
intensity of the bipolar conflict within the United Nations.   The interposition of an increasing number of nonaligned nations juxtaposed
between the two power blocs averts the type of direct confrontation so
conspicuous during the early years of the world organization; more
significantly, perhaps the bargaining power of the neutrals has been
multiplied.

In an analysis of the political process of the General Assembly during 1952-1954, Professor Haas concluded that a type of "balancing"
process among the three major ideological groups was an important
feature of United Nations politics in which the nonaligned nations
took advantage of their strategic position in the Assembly to gain
concession from both rival blocs for economic development assistance
commitments.[5]   In exchange for support of such questions as collective
security action in Korea, the United Nations embargo of strategic
materials to Communist China, and the blocking of the admission of
that nation to the United Nations, Western powers acceded to the demands of the underdeveloped nations for the creation of an International Finance Corporation and the economic development agency
known as the Special Fund.[6]   With regard to the Soviet Union, Haas
found that its endorsement of the Korean truce negotiations after
an initial reluctance came only "after the Afro-Asian bloc had taken
a strong hand in the negotiations . . . [so that] even the Russians stood
to lose heavily in prestige in the prisoner repatriation process." [7]   Thus,
as a result of pressures exerted by neutralist states, the Charter has
been altered by the prominence of economic and social aspirations of
the less developed nations "clamoring for recognition in their own right
rather than as adjuncts to the preservation of peace." [8]

While such concessions to the nonaligned nations may result in
no basic change in the attitude of the superpowers toward each other,
the emergence of a loose and amorphous bloc of non-aligned powers

blunts the severity of ideological conflict as both the United States and the Soviet Union are forced to consider the influence of their policy pronouncements on the neutrals.

Although an inter-regional process of balancing or adjustment of conflicting interests exists in the General Assembly, its influence on deflecting regional security agencies from their major goals should not be exaggerated. The numerous resolutions introduced by the Afro-Asian bloc for nuclear disarmament have not seriously affected the foreign policy positions of the United States or the Soviet Union on these questions. Also, concessions made by the superpowers to the economic aspirations of the less developed nations are not entirely explained by "balancing." They are dictated by considerations of political expedience as much as by parliamentary diplomacy.

Western regional alliances have been nullified to some extent by the development of neutralism. A cursory glance at the composition of the various alliances reveals the absence of a number of key states bordering the Soviet bloc who have declined membership in such arrangements.

Especially conspicuous is the Middle East where the absence of Afghanistan from the Central Treaty Organization and the secession of Iraq from that alliance exposed an important gap along the "northern tier." In the Far East SEATO is seriously weakened by the refusal of India, Burma, and Indonesia to participate thereby exposing a significant area to Chinese Communist infiltration and subversion. For example, if India had been a member of SEATO the Chinese Communists may have been deterred from violating Indian frontiers in recent years. Participation of other neutralist States in the various Western pacts would not necessarily seal off various regions from Communist pressures, but the solidarity of the groupings would be enhanced especially where such alliances include former colonial powers and recently independent nations. As long as such states abstain from membership, the seriousness of the threat of Communist encroachment may lose some of its credibility.

One of the more serious limitations of Western security agencies pertains to their failure to develop military structures capable of effective resistance to Soviet or Communist Chinese aggression. With the exception of NATO, the regional security agencies of SEATO, CENTO, and the Rio Pact continue to function as unintegrated military systems, relying almost exclusively on the protection of the American nuclear deterrent rather than on indigenous forces sufficient to repel an external conventional warfare attack. Initial preoccupation against Communist aggression has yielded to a greater concern for establishing internal economic and political stability.

The shift to internal economic and social development to forestall the revolutionary appeals of communism may be a necessary precondition for increasing the capacity of underdeveloped states to resist internal subversion and revolution fomented from within their borders by external machinations, but the failure to establish integrated defense forces against the possibility of aggression cannot be condoned. Insofar as SEATO, CENTO, and the Rio Pact are deficient in this respect they cannot be said to offer to their participants any great degree of security against less than all out aggressions.[9]

If the participation of smaller nations in these regional systems entitles them to American support in the event of an attack, there is increasing doubt that the United States would unleash its nuclear power unless an ally or allies were subjected to a full scale conventional or nuclear war. Though this is not an impossibility, there is more validity in the view that Communist aggression would be more limited and subtle, culminating in a swift coup d'etat and the displacement of a friendly government by a Communist regime. It was this fear that prompted Thailand's strenuous objections to the proposed withdrawal of American marines after the Laos settlement of 1962.

In a more fundamental sense the efficacy of regional security systems in an era dominated by the race for nuclear weapons has been questioned: [10] "The changing nature of warfare and the revolution in weapons technology pose the final challenge of dynamic conditions confronting the unity of purpose of an alliance. The whole principle of large-scale conscription armies has been questioned by those who see in a professional force equipped predominantly with nuclear weapons the main deterrent to aggression . . . The impact of the nuclear age makes conventional regional systems useless in the view of some critics, while to others it implies the minimization of atomic and hydrogen weapons, with re-emphasis on conventional armaments [to deter attack by conventional weapons]."

A recent example of the questionable utility of a non-militarized regional system involves the sensational introduction of long-range missiles and launch sites into Cuba in 1962 to the consternation of the United States and its Latin American allies. Surreptitiously smuggled into an ideologically deviant power within the inter-American system by the Soviet Union, the buildup of nuclear capability threatened the viability of the entire hemispheric regional system until the institution of a pacific blockade of Cuba by the United States. The absence of any deterrent capability among the weaker Latin American states revealed the inadequacy of a regional security system that gave disproportionate attention to legal and political obligations in time of attack and seriously neglected the creation of military defense forces. In the wake of the Cuban crisis, therefore it was not surprising that many strategists in the United States urged the development of a NATO-like military organization for the Western Hemisphere.

Insofar as the efficacy of NATO as a security system is concerned only tentative assessments may be made. Probably the establishment of that system served as an important psychological warning to the Soviet Union that the West was preparing to resist any further encroachment in Europe. To some extent NATO has proved to be useful for the sharing of defense burdens by the United States with its fourteen allies. But is the absence of Soviet aggression in Western Europe attributable to the presence of NATO ground forces in numerical inferiority to Soviet forces or, more plausibly, to the delicate balance of nuclear weapons that renders any excursion too costly? It may be argued that the nuclear deterrent of the United States rather than NATO ground forces has safeguarded the security of Western Europe. If participation in the alliance for the weaker European states offered an attractive guarantee of self-preservation under the protective shield of American nuclear supremacy from 1949 to 1952, the rapid increase in Soviet nuclear capabilities has made them much less secure and correspondingly decreased the benefits of membership. NATO may therefore be more useful as a framework for the development of common defense and military policies than an effective counterweight to Soviet power.[11]

In an era of rapidly changing weapons technology, some difficult challenges confront the alliance. With the advent of long range intercontinental ballistic missiles, retention of military bases in the NATO area for the launching of intermediate range missiles may be obsolescent since such bases offer less protection against a surprise attack than the largely invulnerable missile-firing Polaris submarines. Even if NATO defense strategy is flexible enough to adapt successfully through increasing reliance on invisible launching sites and the Polaris submarine system, an important contradiction still persists. It lies in the inability of NATO's conventional forces to deter aggressions falling between an all out attack and a very limited probing action.[12]

Solution to this dilemma lies in the strengthening of local resistance forces of the European nations. However, little progress has been achieved partly because these nations are experiencing unprecedented economic growth and are reluctant to divert their resources into the expansion of nonnuclear capabilities. In part the lack of enthusiasm may also be attributed to the American policy of "massive retaliation" as a deterrent to aggression. As Robert E. Osgood has pointed out,[13] "The Eisenhower administration, to the end was adamantly opposed to compensating for the declining credibility of active nuclear reprisals by enlarging local resistance forces. Instead, it remained wedded to the thesis . . . that nuclear firepower would compensate for the reduction of mobilized manpower, and that the forces that would prevent a big war would also prevent a small war, since the chances of even a limited war growing into a thermonuclear conflagration would deter all overt military aggression."

More recently, American strategy has shifted to the development of a more diversified strategy in order to solve the problem of resisting less than an all out nuclear attack in Western Europe by widening the options available. The new strategy seeks to expand the nonnuclear capabilities of European forces in order to cope with limited probes in peripheral areas or with large scale conventional operations in central Europe".[14] "The objective is a force that could hold its own in fighting at the nonnuclear level over a period of time sufficiently long to allow for an agreement by the two sides to pause in order to consider carefully the consequences of escalating the conflict."

Unfortunately, the new strategy has not proved to be acceptable to the European members of NATO, especially to the nations of the European Economic Community. The objections are political rather than military:[15] "just when European aspirations to become a nuclear power are showing signs of feasibility, American strategy is calling for greater conventional forces in Europe and greater control in the United States . . . Is it reasonable, ask the Europeans, to expect one partner, just when it is acquiring cohesion and economic power, to assign the ultimate responsibility for its security to the other partner? Why, they ask, should Europeans forego possession of nuclear weapons when other states may be developing them and the prospect of an arms control agreement seems remote?"

Although the question of an independent European nuclear deterrent is too recent a development to be fully explored in all of its complex political and military implications, recent European interest in such possibilities does demonstrate the dynamic character of the alliance as well as illustrating how changes in the military power of the Soviet Union have produced intra-bloc tensions that are disrupting the cohesiveness of NATO.

When NATO was established in 1949, the United States possessed unchallengeable superiority in the field of nuclear weapons. Affiliating with the United States offered maximum security benefits for the economic and militarily weak European allies who were willing to accept political subservience. Since 1949, however, the Soviet Union has acquired a nuclear weapons capability approximately equal to American capabilities.

Such changes have precipitated a reexamination of the military viability of the alliance in terms of the adequacy of its deterrent power. Despite the presence of American atomic warheads at various bases in England, Italy, and Turkey, pressures for the development of independent nuclear capabilities arose in France under the leadership of General DeGaulle long dissatisfied with what he considered the dominant role of Britain and the United States in the alliance. Moreover, the creation of an independent European nuclear capability has been justified as an additional deterrent to Soviet aggression. Many European believe that the credibility of nuclear retaliation would be maximized if such weapons were not under the exclusive control of the United States.

The contemporary debate in Europe on the desirability of a European nuclear deterrent reflects steadily increasing doubt on the part of the NATO allies as to whether the nuclear power of the United States would ever be used to repel an attack on a NATO state since nuclear parity renders any such exchange suicidal, reducing the likelihood that such weapons would be utilized short of a total war situation:[16]

"As long as strategic nuclear capability was monopolized by the United States and the Soviet Union the lesser states were reluctant to invest in conventional arms. The Western allies did not feel responsible for their own defense as long as the United States controlled the decisive weapon; as the deterrent balance came into being between the two superpowers, the lesser states felt unable to modify it substantially by action on the conventional plane. And eventually they came to fear that increments in their conventional forces might even decrease their security, insofar as a conventional buildup reduced

the willingness of the United States to use the nuclear deterrent on behalf of its allies."

It was therefore reasoned that the security of the European NATO
allies would be enhanced by their individual or joint possession and
control of such weapons as insurance against the possible reluctance
of the United States to come to their assistance with nuclear firepower. Repeated assurance by American officials to the contrary have
not been sufficient to quell discussion of the uncertainty of an American response to aggression.[17] More fundamentally, perhaps, the desire
for an independent nuclear deterrent may be attributed to a growing
European dissatisfaction with American domination of the alliance
in the form of dependency on America for political and military leadership. While this attitude has been most lucidly articulated by General
De Gaulle and therefore reflects French policy, it shared to some extent
by other European statesmen.

The preceding discussion reveals the limitations of an important
regional security system in an era of rapidly changing weapons technology as well as significant regional political and economic changes
that threaten to undermine its cohesion. Equalization of the military
balance of power has reduced the security benefits for the lesser NATO
allies while the economic and political renascence of "Little Europe"
has stimulated momentum for a disengagement from the long hegemony of the great power.

The spiraling of military preparations within both NATO and the
Warsaw Pact systems has been accompanied by a proportional increase in the degree of insecurity which pervades their membership.
This substantiates in part the assumption that an uncontrolled regional competition induces and accelerates international tensions. Though
NATO backed by the nuclear deterrent power of the United States has
discouraged military adventurism in Western Europe, it has not been
successful in eliminating the climate of insecurity which precipitated
its formation or in preventing the accumulation of serious intra-bloc
tensions that have been a constant feature of its existence.

However, the history of NATO does provide valuable empirical
data to test an important variable alleged to affect the viability of alliances. The commonly held hypothesis that the appearance of a severe
external threat tends to promote regional cohesion was substantiated
during the early phase of NATO's experience when the perception of
Soviet hostility expedited rearmament and military integration among
the fifteen member states. That the external pressure of an aggressive

enemy is not a sufficient factor in maintaining regional cohesion is demonstrated by examination of the post-Stalin era where a less hostile Soviet regime intermittently relaxed its belligerence toward the West, provoking in turn a corresponding fluctuation in the solidarity of the NATO system. Thus the essentially negative character of an alliance is susceptible to atrophy if the danger which brought it into existence declines. Unless the alliance can develop positive functions to pursue, there is a tendency for distintegration.

This survey of the principal Western regional security systems does not imply that their establishment and continuation are without value. Rather it points up some serious limitations of regional systems as security instruments. Reflective of the disintegration of world order rather than primary causes of disorder, regional security agencies have provided a basis for mutual defense and solidarity by mobilizing the West to resist Communist aggrandizement. As imperfect substitutes for the universal order that never materialized, they have provided a more certain mechanism of response in the event of aggression, filling in part of the vacuum created by the decline of the United Nations. On the other hand these agencies have not brought the world any closer to genuine peace and security.

Yet regional security is internal as well as external. If the ability of Western regional systems to deter external attack is weak in many areas, what of their success in promoting security through the peaceful settlement of regional disputes?

The theoretical advantage of regionalism over universalism insofar as the peaceful settlement of international disputes is concerned is based upon the existence of common bonds of tradition, geography, and culture. We will discover, however, that this assumption has proven to be false and that solidarity often proves to be illusory when regional disputes arise.

Regionalism and International Disputes. Since 1945 numerous disputes involving regionally proximate states have arisen. If regional security agencies have operated autonomously of the United Nations, there has been little cooperation between regional organizations and the United Nations for the peaceful settlement of international disputes. Moreover, regional agencies have not been very successful in settling regional disputes with the result that with the exception of Latin America, the tendency has been for the other regions to export their unresolved conflicts to the universal organization.[18]

Perhaps the inability of regional systems to resolve regional conflict is most conspicious within NATO, although examples of weakness may be observed in other regional groupings. The history of NATO has been marked by periodic intra-regional conflict that belies the facade of unity it presents to the rest of the world. Many of these conflicts are a product of decolonization or the termination of colonialism.

Prior to the outbreak of the Suez crisis in 1956, the alliance was punctured by the emergence of strong differences among Britain, Greece, and Turkey concerning the future status of the island of Cyprus. Events leading to the termination of British sovereignty over Cyprus were accompanied by increasing bitterness and violence so serious that the dispute was placed before the United Nations since NATO lacked the institutional effectiveness to bring about a settlement. The General Assembly, however, in considering the Cyprus question in 1956 and 1957, was unable to agree on a recommendation for the solution of the crisis. Although the dispute was settled through the moderation of all parties, their common membership in NATO was of negligible significance in effecting a solution. In 1964, however, the Cyprus question erupted again in fierce fighting between the Greek and Turkish communities on the island. The situation has been stabilized by the intercession of United Nations forces, but the future of Cyprus remains an enigma.

Another serious dispute involved the succession of crises between France and the other members of the alliance over the liquidation of French rule in Tunisia, Morocco, and Algeria in which the principle of national self-determination collided with unsuccessful French efforts to delay the disintegration of her empire. Colonial problems not only prevented a more adequate contribution of France to NATO conventional forces; they produced increasing hostility between France and the United States; the latter applied polite but firm diplomatic pressure to eliminate a colonialism in North Africa that was proving embarrassing to the Western states in the United Nations.

Torn between loyalties to a strategically located ally and the principle of self-determination, the United States as leader of the NATO coalition incurred the mounting animosity of the Afro-Asian bloc by abstaining on numerous resolutions condemning the perpetuation of French rule in North Africa. In this conflict the pull of extra-regional interests demonstrated the fallacy of isolating a major regional system from the main currents of international politics. Although the genesis of the opposition to France was prompted by political events outside the NATO area, the severity of the resultant colonial-anti-colonial conflict, its world-wide repercussions on the nonaligned nations, and especially the vulnerability of the Western bloc to Soviet charges of imperialism undermined the cohesion of NATO and revealed its inability to cope successfully with the problems of decolonization.

Despite the subsequent solution of French problems through the emancipation of the North African territories, it would be optimistic to conclude that the divisive impact of extra-regional colonial problems has been eliminated from NATO. The desire by England, France, and Belgium to maintain economic and political ties with their former dependencies still carries the threat of recurrent conflict especially with the United States. This may be illustrated by their divergent policies regarding the unification of the Belgian Congo in 1960. Secession of the Katanga Province from the rest of the Congo brought strong pressures for reintegration from the United States in face of opposition from France, Belgium and Britain whose citizens were financially involved in the operation of the Union Haut-Miniere mining complex in that province. Fearful that such reintegration would result in the nationalization of the mining syndicate, they were reluctant to agree to coercive measures by United Nations forces to accomplish the American objective. Moreover, France has steadfastly refused to pay for the cost of maintaining United Nations forces in the Congo.

But perhaps the most critical dispute was the ill-fated Suez invasion by Britain and France in 1956 that threatened the disintegration of NATO. As another illustration of how extra-regional influences may undermine regional cohesion, the Suez crisis provided a classic instance of the clash between collective and regional security systems. Much to the dismay of Britain and France, the United States placed its obligations under the United Nations Charter before political obligations to its key allies thereby precipitating a serious breach in the regional system.

Invocation by the General Assembly of the Uniting for Peace Resolution in condemnation of the British and French action had placed the United States in a position not clearly anticipated in 1950 when the resolution was adopted at American urging. Designed primarily to mobilize the General Assembly against Communist aggression, it was applied to a situation in which the West was being condemned for aggression. Forced to choose between its obligations under the Charter and its obligations to Britain and France, the United States responded by rejecting the plea of self-defense raised by its allies and supported the condemnation of their action by the General Assembly as a clear violation of the Charter. Fortunately, the withdrawal of British and French forces from the Suez Canal zone removed the embarrassing possibility of enforcement action to put down the aggression.

While the reasons for the failure of Britain and France to notify the United States of the intention to use force in the Suez Canal Zone are unclear, the absence of prior notification revealed a serious disagreement within the alliance regarding the legitimacy of pacific settlement in those disputes involving the vital interests of member states located outside the NATO area. Prior to the invasion Britain and France had been under great pressure from the United States to avoid open conflict with Egypt. Though the action by the United States in the United Nations greatly irritated and surprised them, it is conceivable that their aggression was motivated as much by impatience over American reluctance to sanction what they considered to be a legitimate policy of self-defense as by concern over the Egyptian nationalization of the Suez Canal. Whether their action was explicable in terms of a reaction against long dependence on the United States and the restrictions imposed by such dependence is unclear.

The Suez crisis, however, failed to demonstrate the triumph of the principle of collective security. The United Nations action was collective only in the mobilization of widespread condemnation of the aggression coupled with firm requests for a cease-fire and troop withdrawal; it did not involve collective enforcement action as in Korea. In all probability the fear of Soviet and Chinese Communist intervention and the American refusal to sanction the invasion as self-defense were more decisive in curtailing the aggression.

Further, the Middle East crisis did not reveal the superiority of regional systems as instruments of world order. Although the action undertaken by Britain and France was repudiated by a majority of the members of NATO, the failure of that regional system to deter two of its members from committing aggression was to some extent responsible for validating the Soviet allegations that NATO was an aggressive instrument of Western imperialism. In this connection the illegal acts of two states could not be clearly dissociated from the regional system of which they were a part and served to discredit temporarily the system as a whole. The inability of the regional system to prevent a breakdown in world order demonstrated that regional solidarity may be an illusion under stressful conditions.

The American decision to uphold the principles of the Charter over its alliance commitments may have been based on political expediency rather than any intrinsically greater loyalty to the universal agency. Espousal of the doctrine of collective self-defense would have alienated the neutralist bloc in the United Nations which was strongly critical of the invasion, forcing a closer alignment between that group and the Soviet bloc. More serously, acquiescence in the invasion may have provoked Communist military intervention otherwise restrained by the decision to join with the majority of members of the United Nations in censure of Britain and France.[19]

Regional groups other than NATO yield numerous examples of conflict. The Arab League is especially a system with a large disparity between constitutional theory and political reality. Conceived before the emergence of Israel as an independent state and reposing on the foundations of centuries of a similar cultural and religious tradition and common aspirations for economic and social regeneration, it has thus far displayed only a low level of political and economic unity. Despite the existence of several institutions for the prosecution of economic and social cooperation, the Arab League has dissipated possibilities for constructive regional action in its preoccupation with the maintenance of permanent hostility toward Israel. Conflict between the traditionalist and monarchial systems of Saudi Arabia and Jordan and the republican and modernist systems of the United Arab Republic and its followers is an important divisive influence.

It is instructive to study the deficiencies of the League in contrast to the more obvious record of achievement of the regional institutions in Western Europe. In Western Europe, periodic setbacks to a progressively evolving integration such as the defeat of the European Defense Community and the establishment of two rival trade groups (EEC and EFTA) have not appreciably deterred the attainment of substantial economic and political unity. Though both regions are preoccupied with defense problems, Western Europe has been able to develop positive legal, economic, and political cooperation in contrast to the Arab League. If the reasons for the disparities in regional growth in the non-European areas are not yet clear, some clues may be obtained by an analysis of their dissimilar internal environments. Integration is difficult where politically and economically underdeveloped regions nations pay lip service to the theory of international cooperation but have not experienced a disillusionment with policies of national self-sufficiency.

Only with respect to the collective economic boycott of Israel and the elimination of colonialism from the Middle East do we find evidence of unanimity. With regard to the latter the Arab League cooperated in passing resolutions supporting "Egypt's effort before 1954 to dislodge the United Kingdom from the Suez Canal Base, in the creation of an independent Libya, and in the championing of the Yemen in its repeated quarrels with the United Kingdom over the Aden Protectorate." [20] But it has proved incapable of eliminating several serious disputes involving a combination of factors.

Prior to its secession from the Baghdad Pact, Iraq was ostracized by the other League members for participation in an agency that was viewed as inconsistent with her obligations to the League to oppose colonialism. After the secession, and with an ambitious Kassem government in power in Iraq, that ruler became involved in bitter rivalry with Nasser of the UAR for leadership of the Pan-Arab movement. More recently, the Arab League has been disrupted over the 1962 coup d'etat which ousted the reigning monarch of Yemen. The governments of the United Arab Republic and Saudi Arabia and Jordan have been engaged in a contest of power in Yemen: the UAR furnishing supplies and assistance to the new revolutionary government to preserve its power while the monarchial regimes of Saudi Arabia and Jordan are desperately trying to assist the deposed Imam in an effort to win back control of his kingdom.

Failure of the League to reconcile its various internal divisions is seen as a symptom of its lack of integration and is explained on the basis of a self-contained nationalism operative within the region: [21] "With the exception of the pan-Arab Socialist Renaissance Party there are few ideological links of unity among Arab political groups. Each modernizing elite in power, whether an intellectuals' independence movement or the army, acts and thinks only in the context of its state; each traditional-feudal oligarchial elite is intent on preserving its position and rejects cooperation with hostile groups across the border. They 'integrate' in meeting jointly experienced threats from outside the region; they cannot meaningfully work together on normally integrative tasks. . . "

The inability of the widely differing regional systems of Western Europe and the Middle East to function effectively for the resolution of intra-regional disputes is counterbalanced by the successes of media-

tion and conciliation in the Western Hemisphere where highly developed institutions of peaceful settlement have been effective. Confine-
ment of disputes to the region has relieved the United Nations of their
consideration, demonstrating the validity (at least with regard to Latin America) of the assumption that regional agencies may function
as useful supplementary adjuncts to the universal organization in the
peaceful settlement of international disputes. How can the more successful record of Latin America be explained? This is a difficult
question to answer since the low level of political and economic integration in the region would not normally raise expectations regarding the
efficacy of peaceful settlement techniques.

Until the Cuban Revolution in 1959, the inter-American system had
been favored by its remoteness from the competing pressures of the
cold war. The relative absence of external forces threatening the stability and security of the region may be an important factor for more
effective adjustment of intra-regional disputes whereas the presence
of such pressures in the Middle East in the form of Soviet and American rivalry made that region more unsettled politically. In addition,
the Latin American states have not been troubled with the problems
connected with the liquidation of colonialism. For a number of
Western European powers such problems produced an extra-regional
pull away from regional solidarity.

Of some significance in explaining the success of peaceful settlement
in Latin America is the existence of a greater respect for the legal
regulation of force and the norms of international law than exists in
most of the other major regions. Though the Latin American emphasis on international law may be politically motivated as a pragmatic
counterweight to the political hegemony of the United States, it has
resulted in a rather elaborate structure of conventions and treaties
designed to insure the legal equality of the small nations and to preserve their independence and territorial integrity.

Through the obligations assumed for the peaceful settlement of disputes and the creation of inter-American peace machinery to institutionalize collective action for peaceful settlement, the Latin American
nations have been well in advance of the procedures evolved for the
treatment of political and legal controversies in other areas of the
world. This is all the more remarkable when it is recognized that the
region has had an unenviable record of internal political instability
characterized by frequent revolutionary shifts of government. In the
Middle East such revolutions are also common but they are not coun-

terbalanced by highly developed regional legal and institutional procedures for the avoidance of intra-regional conflict and respect for the
principle of non-intervention in the internal affairs of neighboring
states.

In addition to the more favorable influences cited above, there have
not been any major ideological disputes in Latin America until recently when the Cuban Revolution produced a new threat to hemispheric security.[22] In the disputes successfully quelled, the feudal
oligarchies of one state were involved in minor military operations
against the oligarchies of another state, and the mediatorial efforts of
the OAS were activated immediately to effect a termination of hostilities.

A recent report of the Organization of American States undertaken
at Northwestern University noted that between 1948 and 1959 eleven
intra-regional disputes were submitted to the Council of the OAS for
settlement and all except the Guatemalan affair were successfully
handled by the Council.[23] The successes of the Council operating
through the smaller Inter-American Peace Committe were attributed
to the speed with which the Council acts to quiet conflicts before they
get out of control; on spot investigations to determine the facts; and
a resultant "cooling off" process which tends to restrain more drastic
action by the disputants.[24]

Conversely, a fundamental limitation common to all international
organizations was observed by the authors of the report—the inability
of the OAS to eliminate the basic conditions which precipitated the
disputes and prolong their life: [25] "There has been almost no effort to
change the underlying conditions which initially fomented the strife.
Since such basic causes reside within the nations themselves and since
the OAS in its political activities tries scrupulously to avoid intervention in the domestic affairs of member states, it does not attempt at
present to deal with more than those surface manifestations of tensions
that result in inter-American disturbances."

The report further concluded that the prestigious record of the
OAS as a peace and security system has been over-exaggerated: [26]
"The political-military activities of the OAS are even more plagued
by the problems of national sovereignty than are its politico-economic
activities. The one area of small success is in the development of
legal norms directed toward the prevention of inter-American strife . . .
The machinery of the Rio Treaty has not been confronted by quarrels
among the larger nations; to date it has been challenged only by small

invasion forces and poorly organized ventures . . . Perhaps the widespread regard for the success of the OAS as a maintainer of peace has
been gained only because the record of other international agencies
over the past centuries has been so abysmal."

An important exception to the non-ideological character of disputes
involved a civil conflict in which "democratic -revolutionary" forces
were arrayed against a traditional oligarchy in Guatemala and which
involved the adjacent states of Honduras and Nicaragua. In this inci-
dent the OAS was far less successful because at issue was a state of
affairs (a Communist regime in Guatemala) touching the vital interests of the hemispheric great power that was not susceptible to conciliation.

In June, 1954 the pro-Communist Arbenz government after first
seeking the assistance of the Inter-American Peace Committee appealed to the Security Council to intervene on its behalf when anti-
communist exiles in nearby Honduras and Nicaragua invaded Guatemalan territory. Brazil and Colombia, however, argued that the dispute should first be placed before the Organization of American States
in accordance with Articles 33 and 52 of the Charter, but the Soviet
Union vetoed a resolution to refer the disputes to the OAS. The
Security Council was unable to respond except to pass a resolution
calling for the cessation of hostilities. When Guatemala then an-
nounced it would welcome an OAS investigation team, it was too late.
A change of government occurred in Guatemala before a subcommittee of the Inter-American Peace Committee could arrive, and it
was widely reported that the United States had assisted the intervention in order to eliminate the menace of a Communist government
in Central America.[37]

In an important analysis of the Guatemalan case, Professor Philip
B. Taylor condemned the United States for sanctioning aggression to
present the continuation of a Communist regime in Guatemala: [38]
"The entire situation leads to the conclusion that the United States
failed to give evidence in the processes of the United Nations; that
it dragged its feet regarding effective OAS action beyond the point of
reason; that it was intimately involved in a situation of subversion
of a constitutional government; and that it did not at any time under-
take to make the record clear to the people either of the United States
or of Latin America."

An assessment of the role of regional agencies in the peaceful settlement of disputes leads to the conclusion that regionalism has not

demonstrated in practice what has often been cited in theory as one
of its advantages: more effective settlement of regional conflict than
is obtainable at the universal level. With the exception of the Latin
American system, the other regional entities have not appreciably
relieved the United Nations of considering the United Nations of
considering intra-regional disputes as envisioned by Article 52(2) of
the Charter, Neither has there been any voluntary attempt on the part
of states to coordinate the pacific settlement of disputes on a regional
level with the United Nations as revealed most clearly in the Guatama-
lan affair.

If NATO has been ineffective in settling disputes over Cyprus,
Tunisia, Morocco, Algeria and, more recently, the Congo and Angola,
the referral of these problems to the universal organization complicated
their solution as they became intertwined with the larger East-West
and colonial-anti-colonial conflicts. Ultimately, serious disputes must
in some way be solved by the parties involved since international
organization at the regional or universal level can only apply persua-
sive rather than coercive pressures. The fact that most international
disputes are settled outside the framework of international organizations reveals their limitations as peaceful settlement mechanisms.
Conventional techniques such as diplomacy may be more useful. In
this connection it may be useful to recall that Article 33 of the United
Nations Charter envisages the utilization of diplomacy, medication,
counciliation, adjudication, and regional arrangements before disputes are submitted to the Security Council.

To the extent that regional agencies are inadequate as institutional
adjustors of intra-regional conflict, such adequacy is less a result of
imperfectly developed institutional procedures as it is a consequence of
the demand by individual states of the right to decide unilaterally the
disposition of their vital interests. The survival of this attitude, discernible in the most inflammatory political controversies, obviously les-
sens the efficiency of both forms of international organization and is
basically reflective of the refusal of most states to subordinate absolut-
ist conceptions of national sovereignty to regional or universal peaceful settlement techniques and procedures.

In a world of severeign states therefore a basic limitation on the
full utilization of peaceful settlement devices is their essentially volun-
taristic character under which "no state can without its consent, be
compelled to submit its disputes either to mediation or to arbitration,
or to any other kind of pacific settlement." [29] Despite the fact that

the members of regional agencies have voluntarily restricted their freedom to settle disputes by recourse to force, this does not necessarily mean that they will permit regional or universal institutions to determine the ultimate solution to their conflicts. Paradoxically, the tighter degree of commonality undergirding regional systems is still counterbalanced by the force and vitality of national sovereignty that continually threatens regional cohesion.

Universal and Regional Functionalism. The dynamics of universalism are not limited to military security and peaceful settlement but also embrace the increasingly vital functions of economic and social development. Indeed the basic argument of functionalists is that the relationship between specialized economic and social cooperation and international peace is interlocking and reinforcing: through international economic and social cooperation the very conditions which breed conflict and war may be gradually extirpated from the international environment thereby promoting international peace and security. To what extent has universal and regional functionalism in the period since 1945 realized this assumption? If their contribution has been unfulfilled because of the abnormal allocation of defense expenditures in the budgets of the leading powers, what may we observe about the dynamics of the universal and regional cooperation that has developed?

In particular to what extent does regional economic and social cooperation conflict with or complement similar activities being carried on by the United Nations and its specialized agencies? In theory there need be no conflict between universal and regional approaches to economic and social development. The danger arises in the practical realm where regional functionalism has developed largely outside the context of supervision and control by the United Nation. Inasmuch as the scope of economic and social underdevelopment is universal or inter-regional in character, it would be logical to expect the United Nations to oversee and coordinate regional programs for accelerating economic growth, improving health and sanitation facilities, and promoting higher levels of economic prosperity.[30]

Functional cooperation has progressed furthest only in those regions, of which Western Europe is the outstanding example, comprising highly literate and industrialized societies that have passed through an era of excessive nationalism and possesses economic systems that are mutally complementary. Since European functionalism has been discussed earlier, this chapter will focus primarily on the newly emerging nations where the interaction between universal and regional functionalism is evolving rapidly.

In many of the underdeveloped areas regional cooperation has been inhibited because the level of economic development is so low that all available investment capital necessary for industrialization must be solicited from the United Nations and the wealthier states. National economic planning is not well advanced in many states because of a shortage of qualified economists and public administration technicians. Before successful regional economic planning can be undertaken, more sophisticated national planning must first be developed for [31] "economic development is basically a job each nation must do for itself. No amount of international machinery can substitute for well developed programs at the national level and for the weaving into these programs of all the various types of external assistance available."

Finally, important political obstacles to regional cooperation exist in the form of intense nationalism and intra-regional political rivalries as in the Middle East. Nationalism and political rivalries inhibit internal political and economic stability, making regional coperation more difficult than in Western Europe where more auspicious background conditions for integration prevail. Despite the recent proliferation of economic unions in Latin America and Africa, their viability remains to be tested.

In the face of such internal problems, the underdeveloped nations have sought the assistance of the United Nations and its specialized agencies for investment capital, technical assistance, and economic guidance. The United Nation itself has gradually decentralized most of its economic and social operations through its various regional economic commissions in an attempt to more adequately meet the problems of these nations at the source.[32]

In the case of the interrelationship between universal and regional functionalism, severe conflict and competition between the two approaches has been limited because regional agencies under control of newly emerging nations have only begun to be established. The major problem is the need for a greater coordination of the varied activities of the United Nations and its specialized agencies as well as between these universal agencies and the bilateral contributions of the Western and Soviet blocs in order to eliminate costly duplication and overlapping.

Where regional economic integration has proceeded extensively conflict between the universal and regional approaches is more likely. Although the European Economic Community represents a substantial advance toward regional free trade, the existence of a common external tariff toward the exports of non-European states is inherently discriminatory and conflicts with the universalist ideal of uniformly low trade barriers on a world scale. In part the establishment of new customs union arrangements in Latin America, Africa, and the Middle East is in retaliation against the European Common Market, and unless economic concessions can be arranged between these underdeveloped areas and the EEC there is the danger of an intensified economic protectionism that will hinder to the expansion of world trade. Unfortunately, the United Nations has no control over such developments and therefore cannot function as a coordinator where coordination is so vitally needed.

Concern over the problem was clearly voiced at the Cairo Conference of underdeveloped nations held in July 1962: [34] "Regional economic groupings of industrialised countries will adversely affect the interests of the developing economies, if conceived and operated in a restrictive or discriminatory manner. Joint action by the developing countries themselves can solve many of their problems and will promote more rapid progress on a wider international basis."

Some hopeful steps have been taken recently to mitigate the consequences of European economic integration. The EEC has reduced the preferential tariff on tropical products exported from its associated African members. [34] In addition, a few less developed nations have decided to participate in GATT (General Agreement on Tariffs and Trade) and thereby be eligible for concessions granted by EEC to third states under the most-favored-nation clause of the agreement. [35] Despite these developments, the developing countries are not completely satisfied and are continuing to exert pressure on the EEC for tariff reductions. The situation is especially serious for the Latin American nations who will not have the benefit of associate membership in the Common Market and may therefore find themselves in trade wars with the African states for the export markets of Western Europe.

Regional economic arrangements constitute some improvement over the economic nationalism of the inter-war period though considerably less than universal economic internationalism. The difficulty of achieving the latter ideal through the failure to establish the International Trade Organization after World War II in part prompted the movement toward economic regionalism first in the prosperous and now in the developing countries. Impetus for the proliferation of all regional groupings may also be attributed to the precarious stability of a world rendered insecure by a bipolar balance of power, the threat of nuclear weapons and in the increasing obsolescence of the nation-state as a self-sufficient economic unit. Despite the contemporary trend toward regional security and welfare agencies, some notable progress in stimulating universal economic cooperation has been achieved by the International Bank and Monetary Fund, the International Finance Corporation and the International Development Association, and the GATT. All have been instrumental in developing a wide framework for the purpose of stimulating public and private investment, currency stabilization, and the reduction of tariff barriers.

The case for economic regionalism as an alternative to economic nationalism or universalism has been well stated: [36] "It is more and widely appreciated, by international organizations and individual nations, the more and the less developed alike, that some accommodation or intermediate course needs to be found between the two complementary tendencies that have marked the politico-economic realignment of the world . . . since the Second World War. These have been, on the one hand, the development of global principles and institutions for the direction of international economic relations . . . and on the other, the process of self-determination, through which the currency and trade blocs of the prewar era are being replaced by an ever-growing number of sovereign entities, each with its separate currency and tariff . . . system and all seeking to achieve economic independence."

Within the underdeveloped regions economic justifications for such an intermediate course may be adduced but are less cogent than the case for economic regionalism in industrialized regions. The tremendous expansion of the state system brought about by the emergence of a multitude of new nations in Africa, the Middle East, and Asia may be a fulfillment of the doctrine of national self-determination, but independence has posed a significant dilemma for these new states with regard to their prospects for economic viability and independence. This dilemma is reflected in the fact that ". . . national sovereignty and national direction of the economy are politico-economic necessities but economic development at a satisfactory rate, to the desired level is not possible within a strictly national setting." [37] Under such circumstances regional economic integration becomes a possible alternative: [38] "to permit contiguous nations, predictably uneconomic units by themselves, to join together for certain purposes—and thereby to gain the advantages of economies of scale and intra-regional specialization . . . while still permitting a substantial measure of protection for local interests . . ."

Against these arguments is the fact that at this stage of their development, the economies of the lesser developed nations are not yet specialized enough to permit more than a modest expansion of intra-regional trade through tariff reduction. The problem is that these nations still trade far more with the industrialized regions than among themselves since their economies are competitive rather than complementary. To the extent that underdeveloped nations industrialize and diversify their primarily agrarian economies, the case for regional economic integration becomes more plausible. In the meanwhile, regional economic planning may be a desirable but not a sufficient guarantee of economic growth.

The most critical problem in the relationship between universal and regional functionalism is a clear lack of coordination. An ideal statement of the structural coordination that should exist between universal and regional organizations has been formulated by C. Wilfred Jenks, Director-General of the International Labor Organization: [39]

(1) Maximum use of the machinery and resources of the United Nations system to insure that independent action develops within a universal framework. Regional groups should cooperate on the basis of interdependence rather than utilized as instruments to promote regional nationalism.

(2) Relations between world and regional organizations should be mutually reinforcing.

(3) To improve efficiency of administration, policy-making bodies of regional organizations need to be apprised of the policies and programs of world organizations.

Mr. Jenks also believes that the problem of coordination takes on special significance in Western Europe where as a consequence of advanced integration Europe "may well be the testing ground for an attempt to evolve reasonable working relationships between world and regional organizations which will ultimately be of wider application." [40] If this assumption is valid, then there is not much room for optimism in view of the absence of significant coordinating links between the regional organizations in Western Europe and the United Nations.

The absence of adequate institutional coordination between the United Nations and its specialized agencies and regional economic development agencies in the advanced and less developed regions encourages the emergence of inter-regional economic conflict. Discriminatory elements inherent in existing and projected regional economic groupings could be softened through joint participation of advanced and underdeveloped nations in a economic development agency under the aegis of the United Nations. In the absence of such an agency, economic development and planning proceeds uncoordinated and uncontrolled in many regions resulting in a duplication of efforts by the myriad of multilateral and bilateral agencies funneling aid into the non-Western areas.

Although there is a greater equilibrium in the scope of activities between universal and regional functionalism than universal and regional security systems, the absence of adequate coordination reflects not only the desire by the specialized agencies for autonomy but also the tendency of regional functionalism to operate even more independently of the universal organization.[41] This would seem to be especially true for Western European regionalism. On the other hand, it may be argued that the need for coordination in the early stages of European integration was not urgent since the United Nations was increasingly utilized as an instrument to promote the economic development of non-Western areas. Since the establishment of the European Common Market and the Organization for Economic Cooperation and Development, both envisaging substantial investment by member states in the economies of the underdeveloped states, a serious need has arisen for the coordination of their programs with those of the United Nations and its specialized agencies.

That such cooperation has not been forthcoming is perhaps explicable in terms of the reluctance of Western European nations to contribute large sums to an international organization in which they would constitute only a minority and could not therefore control. Similarly, insofar as cooperation with universal agencies are concerned many European nations prefer to keep it minimal because they derive greater benefits through participation in regional agencies.

The absence of coordination between regionalism in the underdeveloped nations and the United Nations may be explained by the newness of such agencies in the non-Western areas. Cooperation with the United Nations appears likely since the newly emerging nations are less critical of United Nations assistance than they are to aid distributed by former metropole powers on the basis of political criteria. [42]

Some additional difficulties of coordinating universal and regional functionalism may be gleaned by analysis of pertinent provisions of the United Nations Charter. Intergovernmental agencies of an economic and social character are mentioned in Articles 57 and 63 where provision is made for the specialized agencies to be brought into cooperative relationship with the United Nations through the conclusion of special agreements with the Economic and Social Council. However, there is no mention of regional agencies perhaps because the framers of the United Nations Charter overoptimistically expected that the postwar international environment would be governed by universal rather than regional economic and social cooperation. Neither the General Assembly or the Economic and Social Council have specific functions in relation to regional bodies under the Charter. The failure to establish more detailed provisions for the integration of universal and regional functionalism is regrettable and has contributed in part of the autonomy of the latter. As is especially discernible with regard to regional security agencies, nonuniversal functional groups may be competitive with each other and the universal agency to the extent that they are removed from effective control.

Though Article 61 of the Charter of the Organization of American States provides for cooperation between the OAS and the United Nations, [43] "there is no formal agreement between the OAS and the UN as such, although there are informal relationships at the secretariat level . . . ILO, FAO, UNESCO have entered into general agreements with the OAS, which without being very specific, provide for cooperation, mutual consultation, exchange of information and documents, and in some cases, for joint action on technical matters of mutual interest."

As previously observed, relations between the United Nations system and Western European organizations are also tenuous: [44] "While East-West tensions persist, it cannot be expected that close organic relationships will be established between these regional organizations and the organs and agencies of the UN system in which the Soviet bloc is represented."

Coordination between military and non-military regional organizations in the Western bloc has not developed formally. In an exchange of notes between the Secretaries General of OAS and NATO in 1958 there was a willingness to share information on ". . . questions of common interest" but Secretary-General Mora (of the OAS) replied that "the OAS and NATO have separate and distinct natures." [45]

To some extent coordination is assured by the United States as the leading member of a network of world-wide regional agencies, but the ineffectiveness of such informal links is well illustrated by the following examples. Until quite recently the United States evinced a greater concern for and attention to Western Europe than Latin America, engendering within the latter region deep resentment over prolonged relegation to a lower priority in American foreign policy planning. Only recently has the United States grasped the significance of the economic problems that are likely to emerge as a result of the formation of the European Common Market and the Latin American and Central American customs unions. Institutional links are urgently needed as the EEC prepares to enlarge through the inclusion of African states and to discriminate against the export of primary products from Latin America.[46]

Contacts are improving, however, between Latin American regional agencies and the United Nations where formal cooperative agreements have been reached between the Inter-American Economic and Social Council and the Economic Commission for Latin America, (ECLA), the Agricultural Sciences Institute and the Food and Agricultural Organization (FAO), and the Pan American Health Organization and the World Health Organization (WHO).

Cooperation among these entities varies from the keen rivalry of the ECLA and the Inter-American Economic and Social Council to the successful cooperation between the respective universal and regional health agencies. ECLA has played an important role in assisting Latin America to establish customs unions, thereby demonstrating that the United Nations and regional cooperation in the Western Hemisphere may be based on partnership rather than rivalry.[54]

Among the factors predisposing toward greater coordination between the Western Hemisphere and the United Nations are the following evidences of interdependence: increasing economic ties between Latin America and other regions, and the common aspirations of Latin America and the Afro-Asian bloc in the General Assembly. The OAS-UN relationship reveals certain ambivalent possibilities for the harmonization of universal and regional cooperation since "it is as possible to develop an OAS which is competitive and a threat to the functioning of the UN as it is to build a regional organization which integrates into the larger picture." [49]

Coordination Through a World Economic Development Agency. In recent years there have been increasing suggestions for a larger role for the United Nations in the financing and control of international economic development with diminishing emphasis on bilateral assistance by wealthier nations — based on the assumption that such assistance would be more acceptable to recipients if it were free from the "aid with strings" approach. A stronger role for the United Nations has also been defended on the grounds that it would permit a more rational employment of resources if existing international agencies were consolidated into a single world development agency.

We will now examine two such proposals advanced by Professor Stanley Hoffmann and a group of scholars from Syracuse University. The general scheme outlined by Hoffmann is similar to proposals developed by the Swedish economist, Gunnar Myrdal, Eugene Black, former President of the International Bank, and Senator J. William Fulbright.

Professor Hoffmann has advocated a stronger role for the United Nations in order that it may be able to coordinate regional economic development. A world economic development agency within the United Nations would have the power to coordinate and control existing activities of the various specialized agencies in the underdeveloped nations. [50]

The reluctance of the United States and Great Britain to allow the United Nations to play such a role by transfering a major part of their foreign aid funds to the United Nations is based on a fallacious assumption: that the West might lose its freedom of movement on the economic front of the cold war if it accepted a system in which the smaller powers and the USSR could control use of Western resources." [51] Professor Hoffmann argues that the assumption is questionable because: [52]

(1) It is better to risk the right of veto in the UN economic development agency that to "sow seeds of grave economic rivalries, misallocation of resources, social and international tensions by taking no action at all."

(2) The opportunities that a UN agency might give to the Soviets are not greater than they already possess for exploiting the forces of

nationalism in the underdeveloped states.   Bilateral aid programs promote neutralism because recipients wish to escape from the influence
of wealthy donors.

(3) Dealing with neutrals through an economic development
agency would enable the West to more easily control their maneuvers
than in the General Assembly.   To be eligible for aid, the neutrals
would have to fulfill certain conditions and would therefore be under
some restraints.

The United Nations has established a Special Fund to assist the
underdeveloped nations, but it works directly with nations and not
through regional development agencies.   Since the United States is the
largest contributor and the management of the Fund is entrusted to an
American, Mr. Paul Hoffman, it is difficult to avoid the conclusion that
the disposition of assistance under the Fund is greatly influenced by
the foreign policy objectives of the United States and therefore does
not constitute a significant improvement over the frequently cited
objections to bilateral aid programs.   It is limited by the fact that most
of its activities have involved pre-investment projects rather than capital investment.   In 1961 and 1962 members of the Fund made pledges
which amounted to much less than the target figure of $100,000,000 a
year.[53]

The desirability of a world economic development agency of larger
scope and financial power than the Special Fund needs to be examined
critically.   A universal agency, despite Professor Hoffman's argument,
could become a battleground for economic and political warfare by the
superpowers for the allegiance of the neutrals.   An effective agency
operating under United Nations auspices presupposes cooperation between the superpowers which is a condition contrary to fact.   If it is
objected that the participation of the Soviet bloc would not be necessary, then the agency would operate under the stigma of Western
imperialism which the Soviets would undoubtedly fasten on it.   Secondly, the rudimentary character of most regional development agencies
in the non-Western areas would hamper the distribution of aid from
the universal agency.   Planning for the improvement of living standards in the less developed nations requires that external funds be allocated and distributed on the basis of a well conceived regional economic
plan.

The failure of many new nations to develop the necessary national
economic integration and coordination of development planning remains an impediment not only to effective regional cooperation but also

a barrier to universal-regional cooperation. A recent ECOSOC report confirmed this problem: [54]

"The failure to plan properly has resulted in much wasted effort: Tax systems are often structurally and administratively inadequate; the progress of land reform, after political obstacles have been eliminated, has sometimes been slowed by the absence of well thought out provisions for financing the cultivators' initial requirements; a pre-investment venture has been launched before there was an assurance that the means to finance its completion were at hand; a haphazard basis for determining particular sectoral programs led to underestimation of other dynamic sectors. Such errors have contibuted to the often erratic and wasteful nature of development assistance."

Finally, the most serious obstacle to the creation of such an agency is the unwillingness of Western nations to contribute the bulk of their foreign aid funds to an institution they could not control. As long as the wealthier nations are willing to accept the criticism that often accompanies bilateral aid programs without terminating them, it is unlikely that they will abandon a form of political and economic strategy for one which would require the subordination of national interest considerations to regional requirements for economic development.

A more novel approach to a world development authority has been suggested by a Syracuse University report on the operational aspects of United States foreign policy.[55] Pointing to the lack of international machinery for promoting world economic development and to the functional particularism of the specialized agencies and their lack of coordination, the report proposes the decentralization of economic development activities through the establishment of "country programs" headed by individual directors who could have the responsibility for coordinating national economic development operations and in turn be supported by and responsible to the global authority.

Decentralization of economic development planning would provide more reliable estimates to external assistance agencies of a country's need for and ability to use financial technical assistance; "build up the technical capacity, administrative organs, and conceptual framework to enable the country to do the job of development program coordination on its own;" and allow a more rational employment of the financial contributions of each country to the projects of highest priority.

The role of the country director would be crucial. He would have responsibility for coordinating the operations of the international assistance agencies by recommending which projects should be given priority in the allocation of international funds and in supervising the execution of funds allocated by the various agencies.[56]

The global authority would have as a minimum: (a) clearcut responsibility for defining the objectives and operating principles that the multilateral development program should follow; (b) consistent policy and management, not subject to arbitrary pressures in favor of particular natural interests, and with full authority to select its own staff; and (c) strong support of member states especially the industrialized states who would contribute the bulk of resources for its objectives and management. The World Bank was suggested as the framework for such an authority because of its "necessary prestige and sound organization principles, of which the weighted vote, which assures effective control to those nations that have the greatest stake in the world economy, and the very strong position of its President are the most important."[57]

The new world development agency would not bypass existing or future regional development agencies but would utilize such organs as the Inter-American Development Bank, the Colombo Plan, and the Arab Financial Institution "as intermediate agencies between the Countries directors and the global authority for reviewing and co-ordinating programs and allocating funds."[58]

Although the report recognizes the difficulty of establishing such an agency, it argues that such an approach is feasible if supported by the United States, asserting that when the United States accepted the idea of an International Finance Corporation, Special Fund, and International Development Association "other major contributing countries lined up in support within a very few months, or even weeks."[59]

While the Syracuse plan would be an improvement over the chaotic character of uncoordinated economic development activities carried on by a multiplicity of international agencies (though technical assistance programs of the United Nations and its specialized agencies are coordinated through the Expanded Program), it is subject to a number of defects that cannot be ignored.

The assumption that the specialized agencies would permit representatives of a global body to supervise the distribution and allocation of their resources for economic development projects contradicts the tradition of autonomy in which they have been operating since 1945. They would undoubtedly resist pressures that would curtain the freedom of their operations as well as be hostile to efforts on the part of

the personnel of a world development agency to plan economic development programs in cooperation with particular countries. Such planning would involve an encroachment upon the functional jurisdictions
of the specialized agencies and involve greater subordination to a central authority that was envisaged in the United Nations Charter or
which has evolved in practice.

The experience of the specialized agencies with regard to the coordination of technical assistance activities is instructive in regard to
the Syracuse proposal. In this connection it has been observed that[60]
"The specialized agencies only reluctantly accepted a coordinated approach to projects financed under the Expanded Programme; and they
continue to guard jealously the autonomy of technical assistance programs financed under their regular budgets."

Whether regional agencies would cooperate smoothly with the world
authority is also questionable. The Syracuse proposal offers no
guarantee against regional competition for the funds of the global
authority. More significantly, regional agencies might resent the power
of the global authority in the joint planning of individual country
programs as a type of neo-colonialism since the major decisions of the
authority would be made by the Western powers as the largest contributors.

Perhaps the most serious limitation of the plan lies in the invalidity
of the premise that the policy and management of a world development authority would be immune from the influence of the national
interests of any particular state or bloc. As previously discussed in
connection with Professor Hoffmann's proposal, it is unlikely that the
principal Western contributors would be willing to divorce national
and international policy considerations from the management and
scope of the operations of a new development agency. With the likely
absence of the Soviet bloc, it would function as an instrument for the
promotion of Western security interests in the underdeveloped nations
rather than as an organization insulated from the particular interests
of any state of bloc.

Western support would be questionable even with a system of
weighted voting on the basis of the following objections: [61]

(1) "Legislative bodies are likely to resist voting large amounts of
tax money to an international aid organization over which they could
subsequently exercise little influence. They are likely to insist upon
retaining sufficient control to be satisfied that the money is being
efficiently administered and that reasonable criteria for its use are being

maintained." Injection of such preconditions would probably be rejected by neutral recipient nations as a return to neo-colonialism.

(2) With the unlikely disappearance of national aid agencies, the creation of a new international agency might add to the confusion. (The Syracuse plan does not mention the difficult problem of coordination with the bilateral aid agencies. It is unlikely, however, that they would be willing to submit to such coordination which would involve a renunciation of their freedom to use foreign aid to advance their own national interests).

A final limitation concerns the role of country directors. While the decentralization of economic development planning may be commendable in theory, recipient nations may be unwilling or uable to cooperate with international civil servants in regard to program development. Lack of coordination of economic development assistance activities is caused not only by the scattering of these activities among a multitude of independent agencies but also by the failure of recipient nations to resolve conflicting pressures within their various bureaucracies for their own special projects.[62] Unless one department in each state is established to coordinate impartially the receipt of external aid, it is difficult to resist the conclusion that country directors will be subjected to the cross fire of vested bureaucratic interests lobbying for special types of assistance. By rejecting some request they would undoubtedly alienate particular government agencies.

The difficulties of the Syracuse plan for improving economic development administration are not inherent in the proposal but in the political conditions under which it would have to operate. They pose serious problems for the donor and recipient nations alike. Given the contemporary nature of international politics, the Western donor nations could not be expected to contribute funds on the basis of economic or humanitarian considerations alone but primarily on the basis of national and international security objectives. For the neutral recipient states, the establishment of strict criteria for assistance and the intrusion of international civil servants from the West to assist in program development could generate suspicions of neo-colonialism.

Yet the situation is by no means hopeless. A considerable effort is now being expended by the United Nations on a more modest and less controversial decentralization by increasing the powers of its various regional economic commissions on which are represented the states of the underdeveloped regions.

In recent years the importance and scope of operations of the regional economic commissions has been accelerating as the United Nations has become preoccupied with universal functionalism. Originally conceived as advisory in nature within their respective regions, these commissions have steadily become involved in operating functions in the underdeveloped areas "through functional committees, meetings of experts, seminars, technical and economic conferences . . . and establishment of regional standards within global standards in various fields . . ." [63] Theoretically responsible to the Economic and Social Council which may reject their particular recommendations, the commissions have developed an increasing autonomy within the framework of policies set forth by the General Assembly and the Council and have been instrumental in a number of important fields, including economic development planning, the initiation of common market and integration policies, and the training of technical personnel. [64]

The increasing regionalization of United Nations economic and social activities through the regional commissions, whose secretariats have acquired a familiarity with problems at the source that would be difficult to obtain in New York, is illustrative of a gradual trend toward the decentralization of universal functionalism. This has involved increasing contacts between the commissions and the United Nations Technical Assistance Administration especially in Latin America. [65]

As a result of the rising influence of the underdeveloped nations within the General Assembly, increasing decentralization reflects pressures from the less developed nations for a greater consideration by the United Nations of their particular economic and social aspirations. Aside from the advantage of administrative efficiency, decentralization may also be motivated by political considerations: [66] "it was a policy favored by the less developed countries, especially new members of the UN who after gaining independence wished that UN assistance be channelled through regional bodies in which they had special confidence and with which they had special confidence and with which they had a sense of greater identification than with the central administration of the United Nations."

On the other hand, the contemporary trend toward decentralization is being resisted. In connection with a report by experts appointed to study additional methods of decentralizing UN technical assistance activities, the late Secretary-General of the United Nations dissented on the basis of the global nature of the program arguing that "regional administration . . . would inescapably lead to a compartmentalization of programs . . . more expense, less efficiency, and greater complications than under existing arrangements." [67] In addition, while the majority of the members of the General Assembly may be committed to decentralization because that body is largely controlled by the emerging nations, a number of advanced nations may be expected to be critical of further decentralization because it would result in a greater degree of control over the administration of programs by the underdeveloped nations that are largely financed by the wealthier states.

Despite the resistance to decentralization that exists among the developed nations and the natural tendency of United Nations bureaucrats in New York to retain power over the field operations of the regional commissions, it is likely that the pressures for decentralization will continue to accelerate within the commissions and in the General Assembly. If such decentralization is accomplished within the framework of the objectives and guidelines developed by the Assembly and its Economic and Social Council through specific delegations of authority to the commissions, there will undoubtedly be improvement in the overall administrative efficiency of universal-regional functionalism. On the other hand, if the regional economic commissions attempt to acquire the character of self-sufficient institutions, then decentralization would alienate the very bases of support upon which the commissions depend.

Summary. A major thesis of the preceding section on universal and regional functionalism is the need for more effective collaboration between universal and regional institutions to avoid duplication of effect, proliferation of ill-conceived projects, and prevention of the possibility that " regional arrangements might become merely instruments of international economic throat-cutting."[68]. If the latter contingency is unlikely for the regional economic commissions because of United Nations supervision, an increasing number of regional economic arrangements outside the United Nations system may become the instruments for inter-regional economic conflict.

Emphasis has been placed on the desirability for structural or institutional coordination, but this should not obscure the fact that international institutions are not paneceas for the achievement of a more rational division of labor between universal and regional functionalism. In a larger sense lack of cooperation between regional organizations and the United Nations is related to the disintegrative influences of the East-West conflict. The savings that could be achieved by a meaningful disarmament treaty among the major nations could be utilized by international agencies to reduce the increasing economic gaps between the industrialized and developing states. Even if such disarmament could be accomplished, however, the problem of raising living standards and economic growth in relatively backward societies would still be enormous.

Global and regional cooperation for economic development is also hampered by other conditions that are particularly unfavorable. The emergence of so many new nations within the last fifteen years greatly complicates the problem of establishing international stability. As the evolution of the United States and Western Europe from agrarian to industrialized economies was accompanied by an intensification of state power and economic nationalism, a similar process in discernible in Africa, Asia, and the Middle East where the attainment of sovereignty and independence has been followed by unfortunate political and economic instability. The wave of rising expectations throughout the non-Western world cannot be accommodated without expansion of the central authority of the state to provide the political order and stability without which economic and social development is impossible. Unless the manifestations of nationalism that inevitably accompany national integration are directed into constructive channels, close cooperation with international agencies will be impeded. Though much has been acomplished through the technical assistance program of the United Nations, the International Bank, and the Special Fund, "to these emerging countries the elaborate structure of global institutions and principles seems remote and often irrelevant to their needs." [69]

Pursuing policies of political and economic nationalism, such nations are paradoxically dependent upon external assistance if they are to be self-sustaining. Though many of the new nations have been created in a manner that makes them highly artificial as economic entities, regional economic integration is complicated by the intensity of their nationalism and the fact that they trade more with the industrialized states than among themselves.

After a recent trip through Latin America, Professor Raymond Mikesell declared: "Although a Latin American Free Trade Association now encompassing the major countries of South America, plus Mexico, was established in February 1960, my impression in talking with a number of Latin American government and business leaders is that interest in the promotion of inter-Latin American trade is seriously lagging, and that the possibility of expanding this trade is not playing a significant role in Latin American planning." [70]

As we have indicated, however, the situation with regard to regional integration is not hopeless especially if the underdeveloped nations can be taught to diversify their economies and attain a degree of industrialization which will permit them to establish economic complementarity. Progress also will be affected by the general climate of international politics as well as by internal politics of the various nations. In this connection, it has been hopefully observed that "as the emerging countries develop internally and gain experience in collaborating with neighboring nations, and with others still farther away, we can expect their nationalism to be tempered." [71] If this assumption is valid, the contemporary ferment evident in the non-Western world may be but an intermediate stage in the transition to political maturity and meaningful regional and universal cooperation. On the other hand regional clusters may degenerate into narrow and exclusive systems inimical to universal agencies.

Although the discussion has been limited to regionalism in the underdeveloped areas, in concluding this chapter we must not overlook the possibility or indeed the necessity of coordinating Western European economic regionalism with the burgeoning economic regionalism in non-Western areas. Unfortunately, it is unlikely that the United Nations will be able to interpose control over the economic and social policies of Western Europe which is largely independent of the need of assistance from international institutions. In turn this may effect the ability of the United Nations to moderate inter-regional economic conflict as more and more regional institutions are established in the underdeveloped states. Concerted action among the emerging regional economic blocs is urgently needed to prevent trade conflicts that would heighten the antagonisms that separate the Western from the underdeveloped nations, and in this connection, it is hoped that the General Agreement on Tariffs and Trade framework will be utilized for such negotiations as more of the underdeveloped nations are admitted into its membership.

CHAPTER VII

REGIONALISM AND WORLD ORDER

The interaction between regionalism and universalism involves not only an appraisal of their political, economic, and security interrelations but in a larger sense the fundamental problem of world order. If world order is viewed as a normative condition in which law controls international conflict through legal reconciliation and stabilization, what has been the role of regional groups as instruments for the promotion of such an order? This chapter will be devoted to a comprehensive evaluation of regionalism and world order on the basis of the empirical analysis of preceding chapters.

In the context of universal and regional organizations, a significant aspect of the struggle for world order is the compatibility or conflict between regional international law and universal international law. Such a discussion, however, would be incomplete unless it is linked with an analysis of those contemporary forces of international politics which influence the process of law expansion by setting limits on its efficacy; this includes the contemporary balance of power and possible future changes which would affect the structure of world law—especially the influence of nuclear weapons on the balance of power and world order. To what extent, for example, has the discovery of weapons of mass annihilation accelerated the "decline of the territorial state" and paved the way for its displacement by a larger political framework? Also to be considered are the implications of the current disequilibrium between universalism and regionalism on the future prospects for world order. Though the imbalance may be sharpest in the realm of security, the influence of non-military regionalism is also involved.

Regionalism and International Law. As a legal norm, world order is commonly identified with the attainment of universal peace among sovereign states in which law serves as mechanism for the stabilization of international conflict if not its elimination. While such a legal order may be attainable only within a monistic international system in which international law is accepted as superior to municipal law, there is no necessary incompatibility in theory between universal interna-

tional law and the particular international law associated with regional systems. Rather, the coexistence of these two systems has been
depicted as a natural phenomenon in which regional international law
is an adaptation to the environmental particularisms of different
regions: [1]

"There exists a universal international law necessary and common
to all civilized peoples; but beside this universal law, there are particular laws applicable exclusively to certain regions of the world . . . The
historic individuality, geography, psychology, politics, and economics
of a determined region gives birth to a complex of legal principles
particular to the states of that region which derogates in part from
the universal law while implicitly recognizing its existence and its
validity . . . and which constitutes the rational adaption of universal
law to the special situation of this continent or that region . . ."

On the other hand, the theoretical reconciliation of universal and
particular regional law may disintegrate in practice and is said to
justify the subordination of regional juridical orders to the universal
order: [2]

"Regional jurdical order only has sense and juridical value integrated
into an international order. Law is a unitary phenomenon and hier-
archy of norms which find their validity and their obligatory force in
the superior rule from which they emanate. One could thus not
conceive of a regional juridical order contrary to the regulation of
international law, no more than one could conceive of regional arrangements as a source of obligations contrary to the obligations of the
United Nations Charter."

Support for the subordination of regional law and organization to
universal law and organization is not limited to academicians but is
revealed very clearly in the United Nations Charter under Article 103
(1): "In the event of a conflict between the obligations of the Members of the United Nations under the present Charter and their obligations under any other international agreement, their obligations under
the present Charter shall prevail." Article 52 (1) sanctions regional
arrangements for peace and security "provided that such arrangements
or agencies and their activities are consistent with the Purposes and
Principles of the United Nations."

More specifically, compatibility between regional and general systems of international law may exist in various regions where the
relatively undeveloped character of particular international law does
not produce overt conflict with the norms of general international

law, and where such systems develop rules and regulations which reinforce rather than conflict with general international law. An outstanding example of the reinforcing character of universal and regional law may be found in the highly developed inter-American system. Legal principles of non-intervention, equality of all member states, and the pacific settlement of disputes support and complement similar provisions of the United Nations Charter.

However, the most cursory inspection of contemporary international relations unfortunately reveals a very basic incompatibility between regionalism and universalism. Instead of a universal order in which politics is subordinated to law, the world is bifurcated by conflicting regional security systems that function as instruments of power politics despite attempts by the United States and Soviet Union to justify their legal consistency with the United Nations Charter. In actual fact, such systems controvert the spirit if not the letter of the Charter.

To attribute the decline of world order since 1945 to such agencies, however, is to confuse cause and effect, as has been discussed in previous chapters of this study. They are more the consequence rather than the cause of international disorder brought about by the combination of a relatively rigid bipolar balance of power and intense ideological conflict. Yet the continued confrontation of opposing regional bloc systems has undoubtedly exacerbated world tensions not only between the two superpowers but also among the smaller nonaligned nations. The regionalization of world politics has adversely affected the newly emerging nations by increasing pressures upon them to abandon nonalignment. Regional security systems have also been rightfully deplored as menaces to peace and security rather than instruments for its attainment.

Compatibility between universal legal norms and regional international law may also be breaking down in international economic relations where the United Nations is being challenged by the formatio of regional economic blocs governed by principles at variance with the universal norm of non-discriminatory world trade. To the extent that economic regionalism develops into a type of regional exclusivism, the repercussions on world order may be political as well as economic:[3] "regional economic or ideological groups provide no answer to the establishment of world-wide law . . . they tend to promote semi-rigid divisions of moral and economic life and to demarcate the rivalries of the international scene more sharply."

Genuine compatibility of regional law and organization and universal law and organization requires, in the opinion of the author, the subordination of the former to the latter. To assert for the sake of realism than the simultaneous participation by states in both organizational forms demonstrates the essentiality of each and renders questions of moral and legal incompatibility superflous is not very helpful.[4] Reconciliation of universalism and regionalism can only be accomplished by reaffirming moral and legal considerations in order to establish compatibility at least as a normative principle. It is only through compatibility in the real world, however, that any visible world order may be constructed. The concept of world order demands a mutual accommodation between regionalism and universalism if it is to be effective.   ....

Even the most zealous advocates of the regional approach recognize the interdependency of regionalism and universailsm. That is why they take pains to show that regionalism may be an effective stepping stone toward the realization of a genuine world community reposing on a core of regionalized legal structures:[5] "It is necessary not to forget . . . that regional or continental law is a stage toward the universality of law, which remains the ideal toward which humanity ought to move . . . Juridical conceptions must yet evolve very much in order to reach that degree of perfection where all the peoples will accept the same norms and will communicate in the same juridical thought."

Regional groupings, however, are not being linked to form a supranational global order nor is the nation-state being superseded by wider entities except perhaps in Western Europe. Even on the assumption that such a possibility exists, a world order based on the coexistence of a number of equally powerful regional blocs may be subject to the same type of instability that pervaded the classical balance of power system as will be discussed subsequently.

To appraise possible future trends in the relationship between universalism and regionalism requires an intensive examination of three aspects of world politics that are likely to exert continuing influence on the future of the United Nations and regional military and non-military organizations: the revolution in weapons technology; the balance of power; and the interrelations of the three major ideological systems of communism, democracy, and neutralism. Recognition of the crucial role which international politics exerts on the process of the evolution of international law and organization also involves an assessment of the interrelationship between nuclear weapons and international politics since the advent of such weapons has greatly altered the standard assumption and concepts of world politics. Whether the increasing vulnerability of the state brought about by the discovery of such weapons will lead to a revival of universalism is a question that will be examined toward the conclusion of the chapter.

Regionalism, the Balance of Power, and Nuclear Weapons. Throughout the major part of this study, the interaction of universalism and regionalism has been examined in a context in which the existence of nuclear weapons has been noted but not fully evaluated.[6] Such an evaluation is essential in order to place the future of universalism and regionalism in proper perspective. Of special significance is the influence of nuclear diffusion on the distribution of world power. The possibility exists that such diffusion will bring about a "unit-veto" balance of power system in which disparities in national power are neutralized when atomic weapons come to be possessed by lesser states, enabling them to exercise a restraining veto on the actions of superpowers.[7]

Before proceeding to an analysis of the influence of nuclear weapons on the balance of power, it may be appropriate to recall an earlier discussion of changes in the balance of power system and the emergence of regional blocs after 1945. The change from a multipolar to a bipolar international system brought about by the decline in the number of major powers culminated in the confrontation of two great powers in a system in which no "balancer" power or bloc could operate as a stabilizer. Under such circumstances amicable relations even among ideologically similar states would have been subject to severe strain. When in addition Soviet and American ideological hostility was superimposed upon bipolarity, the possibilities for a universal order lessened with the tendency during 1945-1950 for middle and smaller powers to be absorbed into a "tight" bipolar system characterized by profound and intense inter-regional conflict.

After the multiplication of new states in the next decade and their policy of avoiding alignment with either bloc system, the structure of the balance of power was relaxed by the interposition of a third grouping of states between the two major power blocs. Although these states were able to soften the direct confrontation of the superpowers in the United Nations, they were unable to mediate between them and in fact served to exacerbate the instability of bipolarity. Through the uncertainty of their future alignment, they tended to provoke increasing rivalry between the superpowers. How these states will determine the future structure of the international system is debatable. If they coalesce into regional blocs of their own, the balance of power will be affected as well as the universalist-regionalist syndrome; otherwise, the contemporary "loose" bipolar system may continue indefinately.

What are the possibilities for the emergence of a multi-bloc international system and what changes would it induce in the relations between the United Nations and regional organizations? Would the achievement of a multi-bloc system indicate a transition from the nation-state to the region-state? To assist in more thoughtful consideration of such questions, we turn now to an examination of a multi-bloc model of a future international system developed by Professor Roger Masters.

Postulating a "pure" multi-bloc model without the variables of nuclear weapons and differences in the structural integration among blocs, he finds characteristics similar to the classical balance of power model. Substitution of bloc actors for individual nation-states leads to political behavior in conformity with the rules of the older system. Since a multi-bloc system is not impossible within the next few decades, the model devised by Professor Masters constitutes a possible alternative to the present system of bipolar regional alignment.

Whereas many scholars have favored the revival of a multipolar balance of power among individual states comparable to the classical balance of power system, Masters implies that this is no longer a viable strategy with the advent of nuclear weapons since the dispersal of such weapons to an increasing number of states increases international instability. This necessitates a regional rather than a nation-state approach to world order where the number of nuclear actors would be kept quantitatively lower.

Multipolarity therefore is viewed in terms of inter-bloc rather than interstate relations. By his analysis of the behavior of a multi-bloc system under "pure" conditions, we are in a better position to evaluate the familiar hypothesis that " . . . several regional arrangements might in time develop independent power and provide the basis for a more stable world than that which exists today." [8] Finally, when the variables of nuclear weapons and structural integration are introduced into the model, a sounder basis for analyzing the advantages and disadvantages of a future multi-bloc world order is established.

Of crucial significance is the concept of world order postulated by

Professor Masters. As might be expected in an analysis of the dynamics of the balance of power, world order is interpreted "as a structure of power rather than as a state of a structure, such as 'peace' or 'freedom' [or we might add 'stability']." [9] Though it may be objected that an analysis of world order in terms of a structure of power is meaningless unless the purposes of power are stipulated, such considerations are implicit in the discussion so that a rigid separation of the structure from its ultimate ends is avoided. The supposed advantages of a multi-bloc order will be critically examined subsequently.

A basic problem is to ascertain whether the political behavior of regional blocs would be fundamentally similar or different from the behavior of a number of individual states before and after the diffusion of nuclear weapons. Though Masters does not assume that there is a trend toward replacement of the nation-state by the regional state, he does argue that "any long-range foreign policy goals must consider the possible choices between a world composed of sovereign states and a world in which alliances or blocs act as units." [10] In a description of the characteristics of a multi-bloc system, Masters adheres to the premise that a stable international system is not necessarily non-violent or static, but one in which violence and change remain within "tolerable" limits so that the underlying structure of the system is not overturned. Following is a summary of the behavioral characteristics of a multi-bloc international system where nuclear weapons and the extent of regional integration are ignored: [11]

1. Regional blocs may not necessarily be peaceful, but "there is equally no reason to believe that bloc actors would be necessarily incapable of preferring negotiation to war."

2. Four "opportunities" for inter-bloc conflict exist in a multi-bloc system: occupation of territory outside the blocs; through divsion of a rival bloc; by attempts to institute control over a rival bloc; through forcible establishment of world government.

3. As in the classical balance of power system of states, blocs may be expected to oppose any attempt by another bloc to gain predominance and thereby upset equilibrium. Theoretically, where a number of regional blocs coexist, the possibilities for checking a revsionist bloc would be high if the status quo bloc actors were united in their opposition to a threat of predominance. In a bipolar system, any slight change in the power capability of one bloc would be viewed by the other as an attempt at predominance and would be more difficult to offset.

4. In a multi-bloc system regional actors would resist an attempt by one bloc actor to establish complete control over the other blocs in a supra-regional system since this would involve the elimination of the other bloc actors.

5. Though there was no universal actor in the classical balance of power system, the United Nations is included in the multi-bloc model for the sake of realism. Its role is limited to serving as a framework in which inter-regional conflicts may be conciliated.

6. A major difference emerges in contrasting the behavior of an international system in which a number of regional blocs are involved with the multipolar system of conflicting and converging states. In the older system such stability as existed was faciliated by the flexibility of alliances as the main pattern by which the balance was maintained. Freedom of states to switch sides from time to time was a sine qua non of the system. Such flexibility, however, would be largely absent in a multi-bloc system because regional blocs would disintegrate if their sub-units (states) could secede freely. Regional cohesion requires rigidity rather than flexibility.

Under the classical system freedom of maneuver was an essential characteristic of the system where flexibility was facilitated by membership in one alliance at a particular time period and membership in another at another period. Inflexibility introduces a complicating factor into a multi-bloc since "there would be tendency for conflict to be so rigidified that it would involve total war with total aims instead of limited war for limited aims characteristic of the classical system." [12] These observations point to the conclusion that a pre-atomic multi-bloc order would be less likely to maintain international stability than the old multi-state balance of power system.[13] This conclusion will be analyzed in some detail subsequently.

How would a multi-bloc international system operate when nuclear weapons are possessed by several actors? It has been maintained that diffusion of nuclear weapons among a large number of actors equalizes power capability and leads to a type of "unit-veto" international system in which small states with limited nuclear capability exercise a type of nullifying veto over the actions of larger powers: [14] "Any new multipower system will be fundamentally different from the 'classical' one; it will be based not, or not merely, on a chance in the traditional power factors . . . but also on a new development looming on the atomic horizon: the rise of additional nuclear powers . . . It would be radically new in the sense that it would add to the present two nuclear blocs an indefinite number of units which, whether 'big', 'medium' or 'small' in traditional terms would all exist on a basis of fundamental equality as possessors of the new weapons . . . Possession of nuclear weapons as such does not necessarily mean equal power to destroy or retaliate . . . But when any number of uncommitted and uncoordinated units have this power, the situation may be different."

Whether the unit-veto system would prevail among blocs with low nuclear capabilities and loose integration is debatable. Conceivably the more centrally directed and powerful blocs would be able to exercise a greater deterrent power against loosely coordinated rivals, but the latter might exercise some type of veto for " . . . while not having an invulnerable second-strike capacity, [it] is assured that a nuclear exchange with any rival actor having an independent capbility would render that rival vulnerable to a third independent nuclear power." [15]

In anticipation of the above instabilities which would be created by the diffusion of nuclear weapons to indivdual states, Professor Masters advocates a type of "controlled dffusion" to regional blocs in the non-Western areas on the condition that such weapons would not be used for aggressive purposes: [16] "Even if the more advanced nuclear powers should attempt to prevent the diffusion of nuclear weapons and delivery systems, the very process of economic development may sooner or later provide the opportunities for the autonomous development of at least 'minimal' nuclear capabilities. This suggests that rival 'nuclear giants' might well prefer some form of 'controlled diffusion' in which adherence to an explicit agreement not to initiate the use of these weapons was the condition for their delivery. . . . Within such a . . . agreement diffcrent 'giants' might well be understood to be entitled to supply different 'underdeveloped blocs'. In this way the emergence of dangerous nuclear powers might be avoided by insuring that no power has an atomic capability which is too *weak*."

Even if it is admitted that economic development may enable weak state to acquire minimal nuclear capacity in the next few decades, acceleration of the acquisition of such weapons wil undermine the contemporary deterrence system. As long as nuclear bipolarity exists, each nuclear power can devise counter-force strategies for a known adversary, but in a multinuclear system the existence of such strategies may be nullified by the uncertainty as to which nuclear power initiated an attack. Moreover, stability may also be undermined because the calculus of deterrence becomes more difficult the greater the number of nuclear powers. Finally, the assumption that regional blocs in the underdeveloped areas would comply with self-denying limitations on the use of nuclear weapons is open to doubt given the more unsettled character of these regions and their intense nationalism. Diffusion of such weapons could lead to an intensification of nationalism since the disparities of power which have so long obtained between the non-Western areas and the United States and the Soviet Union would be bridged by their possession. The assumption that a multi-bloc system with nuclear weapons is preferable to a unit-veto system in which weapons were possessed by a greater number of units may be theoretically sound, but is a less desirable policy alternative than a policy which seeks to halt the proliferation of such weapons in order to maintain the contemporary bipolar deterrent system.

While the multi-bloc model is a refined and sophisticated addition to the theory of regionalism, it is susceptible to criticisms applicable prior to the inclusion of nuclear weapons as a variable. The following critique is intended as a constructive analysis of its strengths and weaknesses especially as they relate to universalism and regionalism.

As previously mentioned, an important contribution is the hypothetical examination of inter-bloc behavior (at least five blocs) prior to the inclusion of nuclear weapons. For the first time we have a cogent analysis of the dynamics of inter-bloc behavior under circumstances associated with the classical balance of power model. Substitution of blocs for states does not reveal, according to the model, any appreciable difference in the "rules of the game" under which the classical system operated except for one crucial difference—the rigidity of alignment that would prevail in a system in which regional blocs were interacting in contrast to the celebrated flexibility of alignment of individual states. Though rigidity may operate to expand limited warfare for limited aims into total warfare for total aims, a multi-bloc order my be more stable than a multistate system because of more effective deterrence possible where five blocs interact than where five individual states are involved. In the latter instance an aggressive attack by one state upon another presumably would not encounter as large an amount of retaliatory force as would be available when four regional blocs came to the assistance of a beleaguered bloc, thereby increasing the risk to the attacking bloc and decreasing its chances of winning a conflict.

However, in his analysis of the operation of multi-bloc and multi-state balance of power systems, Professor Masters neglects to pay sufficient attention to perhaps the more crucial stabilizing feature of

REGIONALISM AND WORLD ORDER   135

the classical system—the role of the "balancer" power. This feature is so briefly noted that we do not gain an appreciation of the fact that it was not only the even distribution of power among several states which contributed to the stability of the classical system or the modest scale of weaponry and armies. It was the role of the "balancing" power that gave the system whatever stability it possessed. Without Great Britain acting as a "balancer" by throwing her weight to the weaker side of the European balance in the 18th and 19th centuries, the classical system may have been eliminated by a powerful state or coalition. As the most powerful of a group of seven or eight major powers, Britain eschewed political alignment for a policy of "splendid isolation" broken only by periodic participation on the weaker side of the balance. When this role was gradually abondoned after 1900 and Britain joined in permanent opposition to Germany in the Triple Entente, the classical system lost its sustaining arch and began to develop the characteristics of bipolarity between 1900-1914 and later with the rise of the Axis Powers during 1935-1945.

If these observations are valid, it appears that the stability of a number of equally powerful regional blocs would be doubtful without the balancing efforts of one regional bloc. In the event of imminent attack that bloc could swing to the weaker side to make the costs of attack unacceptably high for the aggressor, precluding its predominance in the same way that Britain functioned to prevent any one continental European power from gaining mastery over the continent. In a multi-bloc system in which all states are members of blocs, such a "balancing" role could only be performed by a universal actor of considerable military capability. But in Masters' model the United Nations is a conciliatory rather than a coercive instrument. It would be too weak to fulfill the vital counterweight functions required to equilibrate a multi-bloc system. Thus the multi-bloc approach to world order in a non-nuclear era without a strong "balancer" would offer less chance for preventing the disruption of equilibrium than the classical balance of power system in which the "balancer" operated as a stabilizing feature.

Can it be assumed that the situation would be improved when the variable of nuclear weapons is introduced by the model? As we have previously indicated, the arguments for preserving the contemporary bipolarity are more cogent than the alternative of a multi-bloc system with nuclear weapons. It is probable that any future multi-bloc system would be one in which there were unequal nuclear capabilities unless the "nuclear giants" were to adopt a policy of "controlled diffusion as suggested by Professor Masters. Inasmuch as this appears to be a remote possibility, we must consider the viability of an international system where regional blocs are unequal in nuclear capability. If the United Nations is virtually excluded from that system, then it could not function as a "balancer" among competing blocs. It is extremely doubtful that a universal actor could be effective in a system in which all political and military power were controlled by regional actors.

While there would be less possibility of nuclear war with fewer nuclear actors in a multi-bloc system, the simple renunciation by such actors of the use of such weapons for aggressive purposes is an insufficient and insecure basis for nuclear stability. As long as regional blocs are disparate in their nuclear capabilities, pressure will be generated among the weaker blocs for the acquisition of more weapons as well as among the stronger blocs to safeguard their superiority. With no centralized actor to impose restraints, there is apt to be a relentless pursuit for a "margin of superiority" that may serve to vitiate any self-denying agreements. Unless nuclear stockpiles are destroyed and their future production prohibited, it is difficult to be optimistic about the supposed stability of a future multi-bloc approach to world order. Such action, however, may presuppose the existence of a world state rather than a multi-bloc international system.

Another criticism of the multi-bloc model is more empirical. While Professor Masters' vision of a series of regional blocs in the non-Western areas is a distant projection, it may be questioned whether this assumption is a valid one. In the short run it is much more likely that new power centers will develop within individual states as nuclear weapons are acquired by middle and smaller power rather than within new regional systems.

Establishment of centrally directed regional blocs in Africa, Asia, and the Middle East is doubtful as long as these regions are suffused with the vibrant nationalism that constitutes the greatest barrier to genuine regional integration. Though nationalism may eventually yield to a cooperative regional internationalism and to a type of multi-bloc order envisioned by Professor Masters, the diffusion of nuclear weapons to these regions by the United States or Soviet Russia or their independent acquisition would probably intensify nationalism.

Whereas the two superpowers have thus far exhibited self-restraint as nuclear powers, the same assumption cannot be made with regard to those states or regions which may come to acquire nuclear capabilities. Because of their greater politcal instability and the intensification of nationalism that would ensue from the possession of nuclear weapons, the danger of nuclear war might be accelerated:[17] "So long as fairly stable and reasonably responsible regimes, such as the American, the British, and even the Soviet . . . are the arbiters of the world's fate . . . there is still hope. What will happen if and when our fate depends on a new Hitler, or even merely a new Mossadegh, a Nasser, any new junta or caudillo of the Latin American type? The present superpowers might yet want to cooperate in order to forestill adventurism of this sort."

Diffusion of nuclear weapons to individual states or blocs that do not already possess them is to be condemned as an unrealistic solution to the problem of stabilizing the military environment. Dispersal of such weapons to less stable regimes increases the possibility that a nuclear exchange may be initiated by an irresponsible state or bloc despite the existence of prior agreement banning the use of such weapons as instruments of war. It is too much to assume that statesmen and decision-makers will act rationally under all conditions and circumstances. The only realistic solution to a more stable international order is total nuclear disarmament.

Does the inability of the major powers to achieve even a limited arms control agreement imply that they should accept as inevitable the proliferation of nuclear weapons to other states? Despite the failure of disarmament negotiations since 1945, it is in the interests of both the Western and Soviet blocs to agree to prohibit the export of nuclear weapons to third states, including their own allies. While it may be argued that such an agreement will not end the desire for third states to obtain nuclear capability for their own protection and prestige, a determination by both blocs to refrain from supplying such weapons would at the minimum postpone their procurement and conceivably provide additional time for the consummation of disarmament measures that could discourage the independent acquisition of nuclear weapons. Unless an effective disarmament agreement is reached among the superpowers within the next few years, the spread of nuclear weapons will render the precarious balance of terror among the two power blocs even more unstable as more states obtain such weapons.

Universalism as a Solution. In view of the possibility that a "unit-veto" international system will emerge and threaten the world with greater instability than now exists, a number of writers have urged that the only solution to the nuclear arms race and indeed to the survival of the state system lies in a revival of universalism. Professor John Herz has reasoned that the nation-state has become obsolete with the discovery of nuclear weapons because it is no longer able to guarantee the protection and security for its citizens normally associated with statehood.[18] Under the threat of nuclear annihilation it should be forsaken for a wider unity.

The threat of nuclear annihilation however, may be a necessary but not sufficient condition for the establishment of territorial units wider than the national state: [19] "In point of fact, men's loyalties have been shifted from narrow to broader communities, but rarely has the scope of the community involved such a revolutionary change . . . Herz is forced to argue that the threat of nuclear annihilation must induce this change, but popular apathy would seem to belie the actuality of this process . . . World-wide organization, if it assumed direct powers over all regions and states, is likely to do so under the 'guidance' of a hegemonic power center."

In anticipation of this objection Professor Herz offers the following rejoinder: [20] "What is the universalist to reply to the seemingly conclusive argument that what he advocates runs counter to the vital interests of the nation to which he belongs, that its very survival is incompatible with universalist policies, and that advocating them . . . implies disloyalty to his country? . . . In the vital field of security the old reliance on power is no longer valid . . . survival now involves as least renunciation of 'total' war, and that this renunciation will ultimately mean divesting nations of their nuclear power. Such a divestment would not, however, diminish the status or stature of nations in the world . . . Contrary to what is commonly assumed . . . the realization of this objective would render the 'world-state' unnecessary and give a new lease of life to nation-states."

This rejoinder is contradictory. How can control over a vitally important segment of sovereignty (the right to produce and use weapons) be abandoned without drastically curtailing sovereign power? If it is assumed otherwise, that nations would not be reduced in status by forsaking nuclear power, then we are back once again to the very factors which are the source of international conflict—sovereignty and nationalism.

The anatomy of the "new" universalism which Herz argues is necessary to save mankind from doom is disappointingly vague. We are expected to believe that the horror of atomic co-annihilation is so frightening that " . . . having experienced that feeling . . . we shall then be capable to translating it into something more positive: a sense of concern which will urge us to be alert to chances to prevent extinction." [21] Yet he offers no specific positive program for a "new" universalism, maintaining that " . . . a new attitude would seem to be at once more urgent and more profitable than to engage again in the more traditional and common discussion of a future world order." [22]

While it may be true that a revolutionary transformation of attitudes is a necessary prerequisite for the abolition of nuclear weapons, no meaningful understanding of universalism as an approach to world order is feasible without some discussion of the institutions and methods for its attainment. It is submitted that the logical agency for a revived universalism is the United Nations or perhaps a new and more powerful successor.

However logical may be the case for strengthening the universal approach to world order to prevent nuclear war, the contemporary world is unfortunately too divided by conflicting political and ideological forces and therefore lacks the necessary unifying elements for a new world order. The nation-state may be obsolescent as a guarantor of security and as a viable self-sufficient economic and social unit, but enthusiasm for the abandonment of the nation-state is not widespread. The world may be unified by its concern over the prospects of nuclear war but it has not yet been able to translate this concern into an innovative institutional response which would replace the nation-state with the world-state.

Paradoxically, in most parts of the world nationalism has intensified at the very moment in which the state is unable to guarantee unilaterally the security and welfare needs of its citizens. In Western Europe the nation-state may be yielding to the region-state, but it is by no means clear that such a transformation is inevitable or that regional integration constitutes any guarantee against a new form of nationalism of wider territorial limits.

If the United Nations encompasses an embryonic world community, it is only occasionally the institutional reflection of a higher international loyalty transcending subordinate national loyalties. It reflects the weakness of consensus at the universal level where conflicting power and ideological components operate as manifestations of national and regional separatisms. Where an institutional consensus does prevail in the nearly unanimous support of General Assembly resolutions for economic development, disarmament, and elimination of colonialism, the universality of the human spirit congeals. But in the practical application of universally supported principles is encountered the greatest difficulty in translating the unification of concerns into the responses of reality.

While vast strides have been made in encouraging and supporting economic development, the amounts supplied are wholly inadequate to fill the ever expanding gaps in living standards between the rich and poor nations. World order depends as much on eliminating social and economic disparities that breed insecurity as it does on devising methods to deter aggression. But a concerted attack upon economic impoverishment in the less developed regions cannot achieve full potentiality in an international climate of chronic ideological and power conflict in which the wealthier nations allocate so much of their budgets to national defense needs.

If the world is unable to make the leap from the nation-state to the world-state and if the proliferation of nuclear weapons to more powers is an increasing likelihood, what conclusions may we draw with regard to the prospects for a restoration of equilibrium between regionalism and universalism? Obviously, these two forms of international cooperation will be affected by the continuing importance of the East-West conflict and the colonial-anti-colonial confrontation which will complicate and delay the restoration of a stronger universalism. To the extent that nuclear diffusion develops and increases nationalism within individual states, it too will constitute another barrier toward the progressive abandonment of the nation-state. Moreover, even if conflict between the former colonial powers and the newly emerging nations recedes as decolonization is completed, no end appears to be in sight with regard to the ideological struggle between communism and democracy.

Acceptance of the need for simultaneous universal and regional cooperation and for the existance of adequate coordinating links between the two levels may be important as a normative principle for the attainment of world order. But a world that is divided by conflicting ideologies makes the possibility for equilibrium between the two approaches to world order difficult if not impossible. A revival of universalism and a subsequent lessening of the regionalization of world politics presupposes elements of consensus and cohesion that have been conspicuously absent in world affairs since 1945. Until and unless international politics evolves into a universal system in which the three great forces of communism, democracy, and neutralism can function cooperatively, contemporary regionalism will continue as a manifestation of a world in disorder rather than as an intermediate transition to a new universal order.

CHAPTER VIII

CONCLUSIONS

Regionalism and universalism have been depicted as theoretically complementary but often practically conflicting approaches to international cooperation in the twentieth century, encompassing a wide range of institutional, legal, economic, and political factors. These factors are in turn affected by the operations of universal and regional organizations. This chapter is a summary of major conclusions regarding the dynamics of regionalism and universalism as they affect the struggle for world order.

The persistent trend toward regionalism so conspicuous since 1945 is in part a fundamental and evolutionary aspect of international society whose institutional roots emerged shortly after World War I. Essentially a pragmatic response to the inadequacy of the world to achieve a universal solidarity, regionalism developed as an alternative but not substitutive approach to peace and security rather than as a theoretically superior form of cooperation. Later, with the complete deterioration of universalism after 1945, regionalism developed as a substitutitive mechanism. But if regional agencies have functioned as "mechanisms of replacement," they cannot be charged with the responsibility for the failure of the general mechanism since regional systems only assume prominence as a result of the failure of the universal organization to operate effectively.[1]

Though various theories of regionalism are useful in understanding why more effective collaboration is possible at the regional rather than the universal level, in the evolution of regional organizations there have often been large gaps between regional theory and regional practice. Further, while universal and regional forms are often viewed as compatible in theory as reinforcing mechanisms for the attainment of security and welfare, empirical observation reveals that this compatibility depends in practice on the subordination and control of regional organizations by the universal agency. In the absence of such controls, regional agencies tend to develop an autonomy that not only weakens universalism but engenders international conflict on an interregional basis.

The precise nature of the relationship between regionalism and universalism depends to a large degree on the general stability or instability of the international political environment in which these two forms of cooperation function. A basic appreciation therefore of such factors as the structure of the balance of power, the influence of ideological factors on world politics, the nature and intensity of nationalism, and the significance of weapons technology is indispensable.

If regionalism has been a persistent trend in international organization since 1920, it has been subject to various phases or cycles of development with the ultimate end point uncertain. Whether the dynamics of regionalism undulate in response to the efficacy of universalism or whether regionalism possesses an inherent dynamism of its own irrespective of universalism is not readily ascertainable by empirical observation. While there is a certain parallelism in the trend toward regionalism that followed the decline of the ambitious universalist structures of 1920 and 1945, the evidence does not suggest that the weakness of regionalism results in a strengthening of universal institutions.

Insofar as cycles of regionalism are concerned, the following phases are discernible: the emergence of European regionalism before 1945 arose as a response to the vagueness of security guarantees under the Covenant and excessive fears over a revived Germany; subordination of regional systems to the League of Nations was accomplished because regionalism was not considered a replacement for the League but a second line of defense against aggression; since 1945 the proliferation of regional security agencies has proceeded autonomously of the universal agency because regionalism has operated as a replacement rather than as an adjunct to the universal system.

A basic distinction between the "old" and the "new" regionalism is the emergence of elements of supranationalism in the economic institutions of Western Europe. Operating largely outside the framework of the United Nations, Western European regional cooperation reflects a growing interdependency of thought and action among geographically contiguous states, moving in the direction of a subordination of national solidarity to a new regional solidarity.

Regionalism is a phenomenon whose emergence and evolution is therefore influenced by the very fundamental internal elements that constitute the substructure of regional organizations. It derives its theoretical justification and practical utility from certain unifying tangible and intangible factors: geographic proximity, common historical traditions and cultural heritage, and economic and political mutuality. These bonds my be offset by the existence of centrifugal forces that retard regional integration such as nationalism, fear of great power domination, competition for regional hegemony, and the failure to diversify regional functions.

If regionalism is a product of the interaction of centripetal and centrifugal forces, it is thus a dynamic rather than a static phenomenon. This renders any predictions of specific regional agencies or indeed regionalism in general extremely hazardous. On the basis of contemporary knowledge, however, certain trends appear probable. One of the most obvious is that the decentralization of political power into regional groupings is likely to be a continuing feature of international relations as long as the international system continues to be divided by intense ideological and power conflict.

Reintegration of regional agencies into a stronger and more centralized universal organization appears impossible so long as there is no enduring accommodation between the United States and the Soviet Union. As a continuing aspect of international politics that affects the universalist-regionalist syndrome, ideological conflict is assigned more significance than the anti-colonial/colonial conflict that is likely to abate with the final liquidation of colonialism.

In the absence of such an accommodation, regional security agencies are likely to continue to function as systems of a fundamental disharmony between the great powers as well as imperfect instruments for the attainment of international security. Whether a diminution of hostility will be brought about by mutual self-interest based upon the fear of nuclear war cannot be ascertained, but the experience of fruitless disarmament sessions since 1945 lends little support to the belief that the emergence of a new age of horror weapons and national vulnerability will in and of itself lead to a reduction of international tensions.

A more fundamental and difficult question is whether the normalization of relations between the major ideological systems would foster a closer relationship between the United Nations and regional agencies as implied above. Several speculative answers are possible. One is that a voluntary accommodation between the Soviet and American blocs may take different forms and have different implications. Depending upon the nature of the rapprochement, national sovereignty may or may not be affected. If such an accommodation simply involves appropriate agreements to refrain from the diffusion of nuclear

weapons, and is accompanied or preceded by solutions to such outstanding problems as Berlin and the reunification of Germany, then
national sovereignty will have been little impaired. The cold war
would continue but within more tolerable limits and lesser risks to
the survival of the nation-state. Under such arrangements, it is
probable that the United Nations would continue to pay a minimal
role in the enforcement of peace and security and that the disequilibrium between universalism and regionalism would not be significantly
affected.

In the rather unlikely event that arms control measures can be
achieved with international inspection and control procedures, the
United Nations may be revived as an instrument of world order and
regional agencies conceivably could be reintegrated into the universal
system for the purpose of implementing arms control agreements at
the regional level. Such a reversal of the historical failure of disarmament negotiations, however, presupposes the elimination of mutual
suspicion and distrust that does not appear probable unless there is
a fundamental realignment of conflicting ideological ystems that would
blur their differences. Such a realignment has been suggested in a
recent study of the psychology of Soviet and American myth systems
in which the opposing systems come to resemble each other politically
and economically.[2]

However, the future of regionalism will not be exclusively determined by the United States and the Soviet Union. Even on the
assumption that a normalization of relations is possible and an increasingly significant role for the United Nations is also possible, it
does not necessarily follow that regional agencies will necessarily be
more amenable to control by the universal organization. Regional
systems may proliferate in the non-western areas and develop as
rivals to the American and Soviet blocs, displaying a similar autonomy
to the world organization. These is also the possibility that a Communist Chinese bloc of Asian states may arise to challenge the older
bloc systems.

The future relationship between the two forms will also be influenced
by the world balance of power especially the influence of nuclear
weapons and their diffusion to more states. Regionalism and universalism have operated in dissimilar environments of power distribution and weapons technology which may help to explain the variations
in equilibrium from the League of Nations to the United Nations.

From 1920 to 1945 the state system was largely dominated by the

European powers in an era in which the universal agency was severely hampered by the absence of the non-European states of Russia, Japan, and the United States. Unlike the contemporary period which has seen the rise of new states in Africa, the Middle East, and Asia, the dynamics of regionalism and universalism were narrowed in geographic scope and a degree of coordination between the two approaches was insured by the simultaneous participation of the leading regional powers in the League.

Moreover, during the League of Nations era a complex distribution of power existed among five or six states all relatively equal in strength. The possibility that rigidified alliance structures would develop was prohibited by a certain flexibility that has been notoriously absent since 1945. As a response to the uncertain collective security guarantees of the Covenant, European regionalism never achieved the significance that has been characteristic of the post-World War II period because it was designed to reinforce rather than substitute for the world organization.

After the emergence of a bipolar balance of power and the discovery of nuclear weapons, the nature of the relationship between universalism and regionalism shifted. Regional agencies became substituitive mechanisms for security as replacements for a discredited universalism. Rival blocs confronted each other with such belligerency that they became possible instruments for the prosecution of nuclear warfare.

Whether the regional approach to international security is as effective as has been commonly assumed is also questionable. No doubt there is logic in the theory that a group of states unified for joint defense may exercise a greater deterrence against aggression than a single state acting alone. Yet even where a strong degree of military integration exists as in NATO and the Warsaw Pact system, we find that because of the approximate parity in nuclear power of both blocs neither has been able to obtain the margin of superior strength that is implicit in regional theory.

In this connection the premise that the establishment of new regional centers of power would constitute a gain for world order by shifting the balance of power away from bipolarity toward multipolarity and hence toward greater stability is dubious. Not only is such a development improbable in the forseeable future because of the absence of integrated non-Western communities, but it may also be undesirable as a policy goal if such regions ever obtain their own nuclear capabilities. While diffusion of nuclear weapons to a limited number of blocs rather than to an expanding number of individual states may be preferable in theory, the coexistence of five or more regionally integrated and nuclear armed blocs offers less stability than the contemporary bipolarity. Not only would the numerical possibility of nuclear war be increased and mutual deterrence complicated as a result of this increase, but the capacity of new nuclear states or blocs to be as self-restrained in the use of such weapons cannot be assumed.

The only possible viable world order based on regional blocs would be one in which the manufacture of nuclear weapons were prohibited, existing stockpiles destroyed or entrusted to a universal agency under strict controls, and the regional systems were adequately controlled by a revitalized universal organization. None of these are realistic possibilities, however, given the contemporary patterns of international politics.

Thus contemporary confrontation of antagonistic bloc systems threatens not only the survival of such systems but the world community. The weakness of the universal organization to cope with the "balance of terror" symbolizes the profound transformation of universalism that renders it incapable of exercising the functions of control and coordination of regional groups described in the United Nations Charter. If the United Nations, however, has proved incapable of controlling regional autonomy, conflicting regional blocs have contributed very little to the attainment of international order. Though the contemporary drift to regionalism is symptomatic of the disorder that has pervaded international relations since 1945, it has also contributed to the perpetuation and intensification of the deeper conflict that it reflects.

Whereas the sharpest clash between regionalism and universalism has occurred in the field of security, the situation is far from satisfactory with regard to the numerous regional economic and social agencies that have arisen since 1945. Arising in part out of the need for security in a divided world and in part as a response to the increasing inability of the nation-state to function as a self-contained economic and social unit, regional functionalism reveals a similar autonomy toward the universal agency though the consequences may not be as distressing as in the case of regional security systems armed with nuclear weapons.

A significant improvement in the coordination of regional and universal functionalism is required if material and human resources are to be mobilized effectively to reduce the ever widening gap between

the advanced and the underdeveloped states. Universal functionalism
of course has been severly hampered by the unsatisfactory international climate. While contributions to the newer nations channeled
through universal agencies have aided economic and social development, the amounts supplied have been indequate to meet their expanding needs and increasing populations.

Though regional functionalism is emerging in the non-Western
areas, regional economic institutions will be unable to function without supplementary assistance from bilateral and multilateral agencies.
Economic integration in the less developed areas is not likely to proceed as rapidly or as effectively as in Western Europe because of nationalism and lack of regional economic complementarity. Nevertheless,
the poorer nations may find regional frameworks useful for planning
and coordinating their economic development policies and for achieving a modest expansion of intra-regional trade.

The commonly held assumption that regionalism is a transitional
phase away from the nation-state is not substantiated by the record
of regional agencies either before or since 1945. Though regional security and welfare agencies may exhibit a greater cohesion than the
United Nations, they have yet to develop structures that reflect the
displacement of the nation-state; and while this may appear to be even-
tuating within Western Europe as elements of supranationalism take
root in economic sectors, it is still too premature to predict that a
regional policy will emerge. A basic retarding factor toward the attainment of political community transcending the nation-state continues to be the narrow scope of numerous regional agencies whose
single-purpose function may inhibit integration: [3] "It is necessary to
banish all hypotheses that try to establish regional arrangements upon
a single element of regional solidarity. Whether one speaks of a
customs union or [treaty] of mutual assistance, they will fail to the
extent that they are not based on different elements which are interconnected."

The preceding analysis of the limitations of regionalism does not
imply that regional agencies have not been useful. Regionalism is an
inescapable political fact as well as an increasingly attractive alternative to nationalism and universalism throughout the world. Regional
groupings established by the United States and its allies have undoubtedly increased the will of a number of nations to resist the possible subversion and overthrow of their political systems and have
brought about in varying degrees a coordination of military and politi-

cal strategies against the Soviet bloc that would have been difficult
to manage in the absence of a formal institutional framework. To an
even greater degree the same positive advantage may be attributed to
regionalism (if that is the proper term) in the Soviet bloc. Achieve-
ments of a number of agencies in Western Europe have been notable
in expanding the focus of traditional interstate cooperation beyond the
nation-state to the concept of a regional community.

To the extent that regional cooperation provides for an increase
in regional stability by removing historical rivalries, settling intra-regional disputes, and facilitating economic and social cooperation, it
serves as a useful organizational mechanism for regional peace and
order by sublimating regional power politics into constructive channels. But in and of itself regionalism as an approach to world order is
incomplete. Regional entities cannot isolate themselves and hope to
survive in a world rendered drastically small by modern communications and technology and awesomely threatened by the specter of
nuclear war. In a world of increasing interdependency, regionalism is
only a partial solution to problems whose ramifications if not their
origins are universal. Unless regional units are controlled and equilibrated by a universal agency, they are apt to lapse into a regional particularism that can only impede rather than promote the attainment of
a more orderly world.

Regionalism flourished under the League of Nations but never
preempted the position of the universal organization. In the contemporary period in which statesmen more carefully planned a compromise between the two approaches, regionalism has come to dominate
rather than play a role subordinate to the United Nations. It is likely
that the future relationship " . . . is perhaps not a problem to be solved,
but rather a process to be managed".⁴ Unfortunately, the process of
managing regionalism and universalism is itself a fundamental problem
inherent in a decentralized system of independent and sovereign states
recognizing no higher law than their own national interest.

REFERENCES

I

1. Inis L. Claude, Jr., *Swords into Plowshares: The Problems and Progress of International Organization*, 2nd edition, (New York: Random House, 1959), p. 275.

II

1. John Stoessinger, *The Might of Nations* (New York: Random House, 1961), p. 338.
2. See B. Bhoutros-Ghali, *Contribution a L'Etude Des Entes Regionales* (Paris, 1949); Inis L. Claude, *Swords into Ploughshares: The Problems and Progress of International Organization, 2nd edition.* (New York, 1959); Clyde Eagleton, *International Government*, 3rd edition, (New York, 1957); George Liska, *International Equilibrium* (Cambridge, 1957); Norman J. Padelford, "Regional Organizations and the United Nations," *International Organization* 8 (1954); Pitman B. Potter, "Universalism versus Regionalism," *American Political Science Review* 37 (1943); Pierre Vellas, *Le Regionalisme Internationale et L'Organisation Des Nations Unies* (Paris, 1948); J. M. Yepes, Les Accords Regionaux et Le Droit International, *Recueil Des Cours* 71 (1947); Commission to Study the Organization of Peace, *Regional Arrangements for Security and the United Nations* (New York, 1953).
3. Claude, *op. cit.*, pp. 111-112.
4. Potter, *op. cit.*, p. 852.
5. Padelford, *op. cit.*, pp. 206-207.
6. Vellas, *op. cit.*, p. 27.
7. Commission to Study the Organization of Peace, *op. cit.*, pp. 27-32.
8. *Ibid.*, p. 27.   9. *Ibid.*, p. 28.   10. *Ibid.*
11. *Ibid.*, p. 29.   12. *Ibid.*
13. Liska, *op. cit.*, p. 143, 148-161.
14. See my study "The East-West Trade Control Program: A Defense of the Battle Act" (unpublished Doctoral dissertation, The American University, Washington, D. C., 1956).
15. *Ibid.*, p. 38.
16. Many scholars and statesmen have propounded this view.
17. Commission to Study the Organization of Peace, *op. cit.*, p. 30.
18. *Ibid.*   19. Liska, *op. cit.*, p. 13.   20. *Ibid.*
21. *Ibid.*   22. *Ibid.*, p. 14.   23. *Ibid.*, p. 15.
24. *Ibid.*, p. 17.   25. *Ibid.*, p. 133.   26. *Ibid.*, p. 134.
27. *Ibid.*   28. Claude, *op. cit.*, p. 113.
29. Norman J. Padelford, "Recent Developments in Regional Organizations," *Proceedings of the American Society of International Law*, April 28-30, 1955, p. 25.
30. E. N. Van Kleffens, "Regionalism and Political Pacts," *American Journal of International Law*, October, 1949, p. 669.
31. Claude, *op. cit.*, p. 113.
32. *Ibid.*   33. *Ibid.*   34. Potter, *op. cit.*, p. 862.
35. Liska, *op. cit.*, p. 135.   36. *Ibid.*, p. 137.

150

37. This discussion is based on B. Bhoutros-Ghali, *Contribution a L'Etude Des Ententes Regionales* (Paris, 1949).

38. *Ibid.*, p. 228.   39. *Ibid.*, p. 32.   40. *Ibid.*, p. 42.   41. See p. 13.

42. Padelford, *op. cit.*, p. 211.

43. Bhoutros-Ghali, *op. cit.*, p. 79.

44. *Ibid.*, p. 101.

45. Ernst B. Haas, *The Uniting of Europe* (Stanford: Stanford University Press, 1958), pp. xiii-xiv.

46. Bhoutros-Ghali, *op. cit.*, p. 107.

47. See Karl Deutsch et al, *Political Community and the North Atlantic Area* (Princeton: Princeton University Press, 1957), pp. 1-21.

48. The chief impediment would appear to be nationalistic tendencies by one or more member states.

49. J. M. Yepes, "Les Accords Regionaux et Le Droit International," *Recueil Des Cours* 71 (1947), p. 256.

50. Liska, *op. cit.*, pp. 142-148.

51. For an informed discussion of the problem of economic regionalism in the underdeveloped areas see Lincoln Gordon, "Economic Regionalism Reconsidered," *World Politics*, January, 1961, pp. 231-254.

52. Liska, *op. cit.*, p. 148.   53. Claude, *op. cit.*, p. 114.

54. See E. H. Carr, *The Twenty Years Crisis* (London: Macmillan, 1946), pp. 228-231 and Walter Lippmann, *U. S. War Aims* (Boston: Little, Brown and Company, 1944), pp. 80-85.

55. Liska, *op. cit.*, p. 149.   56. *Ibid.*

57. Winston Churchill, *The Hinge of Fate* (Boston: Houghton-Mifflin, 1950), pp. 711-712.

59. Liska, *op. cit.*, p. 150.   60. *Ibid.*, p. 152.   61. *Ibid.*

62. *Ibid.*, p. 154.   64. *Ibid.*, p. 160.   65. *Ibid.*, p. 159.

66. Ernst B. Haas, "European and International Integration," *International Organization*, Summer, 1961, pp. 391-392.

67. *Ibid.*, p. 392.

68. Inis L. Claude, "The United Nations and the Use of Force," *International Conciliation*, March, 1961, pp. 367-368.

69. Inis L. Claude, "The Containment and Resolution of Disputes," in Francis Wilcox and H. Field Haviland (editors), *The United States and the United Nations* (Baltimore: Johns Hopkins Press, 1961), p. 116 and ff.

70. The following discussion is based on Harold Guetzkow, "Isolation and Collaboration: A Partial Theory of Inter-Nation Relations," *Journal of Conflict Resolution*, March, 1957, pp. 48-68.

71. *Ibid.*, p. 51.   72. *Ibid.*, p. 64.

74. Alexander Dallin, "The Soviet View of the UN," *International Organization*, Winter 1962, p. 27.

75. Guetzkow, *op. cit.*, p. 62.   76. *Ibid.*, pp. 62-63.

III

1. Liska, *op cit.*, p. 134.

2. Robert Osgood, "Woodrow Wilson, Collective Security, and the Lessons of

History," in Earl Latham, Editor, *The Philosophy of Woodrow Wilson* (Chicago: University of Chicago Press, 1958), p. 189.

3. Cited by Frederick L. Schuman, *International Politics*, Sixth Edition, (New York: McGraw-Hill, 1958), p. 212.

4. F. P. Walters, *A History of the League of Nations* (London: Oxford University Press, 1952), p. 55.

5. *Ibid.*, p. 350.   6. *Ibid.*, p. 395.

7. Bhoutros-Ghali, *op. cit.*, p. 113.

8. *Ibid.*, pp. 116-117.

9. Frederick H. Hartmann, *Basic Documents of International Relations* (New York: McGraw-Hill, 1951), p. 88.

10. Cited in Daniel Cheever and H. Field Haviland, Jr., *Organizing for Peace* (New York: Houghton-Mifflin, 1954), p. 116.

11. Bhoutros-Ghali, *op. cit.*, pp. 119-20.

12. G. M. Gathorne-Hardy, *A Short History of International Affairs*, Fourth Edition, (London: Oxford University Press, 1950), p. 68.

13. Linden A. Mander, *Foundations of Modern World Society*, Second Edition, (Stanford: Stanford University Press, 1947), p. 65.

14. Norman D. Palmer and Howard C. Perkins, *International Relations*, Second Edition, (Boston: Houghton-Mifflin, 1957), p. 340.

15. Gathorne-Hardy, *op. cit.*, p. 76.

16. E. H. Carr, *International Relations Between the Two World Wars* (London: Macmillan and Company, 1955), p. 97.

17. Yepes, *op. cit.*, p. 263.   18. Carr, *op. cit.*, p. 42.   19. *Ibid.*

21. Gathorne-Hardy, *op. cit.*, p. 371.   22. Carr *op. cit.*, p. 213.

20. Mander, *op. cit.*, p. 149.

23. For a more detailed discussion see the following: John C. Dreier, *The Organization of American States and the Hemisphere Crisis* (New York: Harper and Row, 1962); M. Margaret Ball, *The Problem of Inter-American Organization* (Stanford: Stanford University Press, 1944); Charles G. Fenwick, *The Inter-American Regional System* (New York; Macmillan, 1949) and J. Lloyd Mecham, *The United States and Inter-American Security* 1889-1960 (Austin: University of Texas Press, 1962).

24. Charles Martin, "Universalism and Regionalism in International Law and Organization," in *Cursos Monograficos* Vol. VII (Havana: Academia Interamericana de Derecho Comparado E Internacional, 1959), p. 386.

25. Walters, *op. cit.*, p. 394.   26. *Ibid.*

27. Gathorne-Hardy, *op. cit.*, p. 210.

28. Mander, *op. cit.*, p. 79.   29. Walters, *op. cit.*, p. 526.

30. Carleton J. H. Hayes, *A Political and Cultural History of Modern Europe*, Vol. II (New York: Macmillan, 1937), p. 1047. For a description of the spread of nationalism during the period to all parts of the globe see also pp. 1048-1089.

31. Liska, *op. cit.*, p. 147.

IV

1. For a detailed analysis of the discussions on regionalism at the Conference see Ruth B. Russell, *A History of the United Nations Charter* (Washington: Brookings Institution, 1958), pp. 688-712. See also for a briefer account the analysis by Alberto

Lleras-Camargo, the Colombian delegate to Committee III on Regional Arrangements of the Conference, "Regionalism and the International Community," in *Perspectives on Peace 1910-1960* (New York: Frederick A. Praeger, 1960), pp. 107-119.

2. A Colombian delegate to the Conference stated ". . . when the great powers met in October, 1944 at Dumbarton Oaks to discuss plans for the future of international society, they were morally and politically obligated to accept in advance the assumption of regionalism. Without that, it was very doubtful that the 21 republic would have consented to sign the UN [Charter]." Yepes, *op. cit.,* pp. 271-272. Section C of Chapter VIII of the Dumbarton Oaks Proposals recognized the legitimacy of regional arrangements and, with modifications, became Articles 52, 53, and 54 of the Charter.

3. Leland M. Goodrich and Edvard Hambro, *Charter of the United Nations; Commentary and Documents,* Second edition (Boston: World Peace Foundation, 1949), p. 297.

4. *Ibid.,* p. 299.

5. Cited by L. Larry Leonard, *International Organization* (New York: McGraw-Hill, 1951), p. 298.

6. Senator Arthur Vandenberg, who was the United States representative on Committee III, summarized the problem that emerged during the debates in this way: "It speedily developed that not only are the South Americans hot about protecting Chapultepec, but the Australians are equally anxious not to be left unprotected in their far corner of the earth. They want liberty of regional action if some one of the Big Powers vetoes. Other potential regional groups are forming and they could be highly dangerous—particularly the Arabian bloc in its impact on Palestine. Our great problem is to find a *rule* which protects legitimate existing regional groups (like Pan-Am) without opening up the opportunity for regional balance-of-power groups." Cited in Russell, *op cit.,* p. 695.

7. Professor Norman Padelford cites a statement made by the Chairman of the Conference Committee that formulated Article 51 to the effect that while there is no mention of ". . . regional arrangements or agencies as such, it is self-evident that the members of a regional security pact are as entitled to act together in individual or collective self-defense as are any other states." Norman J. Padelford, "Regional Organization and the United Nations," *International Organization,* No. 2, 1954, p. 214. This is not, however, the only possible interpretation of Article 51.

8. Goodrich and Hambro, *op. cit.,* p. 302. Note also the corroborative opinion of Professor Julius Stone who maintans that "in any major conflict . . . at least one permanent member would be interested in preventing the Council taking . . . [enforcement] measures . . . The war could then legally run its full course without United Nations action." *Legal Controls of International Conflict* (New York: Rinehart and Company, Inc., 1959), p. 245.

9. Stone, *op. cit.,* p. 246.   10. Claude, *op. cit.,* p. 121.

11. Goodrich and Hambro, *op. cit.,* p. 309.

12. Norman J. Padelford, "Recent Developments in Regional Organization," *Proceedings of the American Society of International Law,* April 28-30, 1955, p. 20.

13. Goodrich and Hambro, *op. cit.,* p. 311.   14. *Ibid.,* p. 314.

15. Martin, *op. cit.,* pp. 390-391. One authority goes so far as to argue that "the notion of a dispute whose prolongation is susceptible of menacing the peace, that permits the intervention of the Security Council, is a criterion so imprecise that it will permit

the Security Council continuous intervention even in regional negotiations." The interests then of the disputants will be sacrificed in favor of an agreement endorsed by the great powers. Bhoutros-Ghali, *op. cit.*, p. 165, pp. 182-183. Fortunately, this theory has not been validated in those disputes involving the attention of both the United Nations and regional agencies.

16. Brookings Institution, *Major Problems of United States Foreign Policy 1951-1952* (Washington: Brookings Institution, 1952), p. 361. Senator Vandenberg explained that " . . . this exception was based upon the conviction that existing instruments for the permanent and effective demilitarization and control of the enemy states should be utilized to the fullest extent, until such time as it should prove mutually agreeable, both to the Organization and to the governments concerned, that the Organization should take over the responsibility. The failure to establish any permanent control over the ex-enemy states was one of the tragedies following the first World War. It was essential not to repeat this error." Cited by Russell, *op. cit.*, p. 710.

17. Stone, *op. cit.*, p. 252.

18. Norman J. Padelford, "Regional Organization and the United Nations," *op. cit.*, p. 213.

19. Professor Yepes argues that contrary to various opinions Article 54 was not intended to enable the United Nations to control regional arrangements but to be kept apprised of their activities. *op. cit.*, p. 281. It is difficult, however, to see how the furnishing of information does not constitute a type of control especially where such information is political and military in character.

20. Leonard, *op. cit.*, pp. 302-303.

21. See the editorial note of Hans Kelsen in the *American Journal of International Law*, January, 1951, in which he argues that collective self-defense agencies may be classified as regional arrangements (p. 163, 165). The same author in his *Law of the United Nations* (1950) asserted that as a result of the paralysis of the Security Council Article 51 "may play a greater role that it might be expected to play within an organization whose main purpose is to make the exercise of this right superflous." p. 804.

22. W. W. Kulski, "The Soviet System of Collective Security Compared with the Western System," *American Journal of International Law*, July, 1950, p. 463.

23. Goodrich and Hambro, *op. cit.*, p. 302.

24. Stone, *op. cit.*, pp. 247-248.

25. Claude, *op. cit.*, p. 275. He uses NATO as an example of a regional treaty for selective rather than collective security.

26. Stone, *op. cit.*, p. 265.

27. Francis Wilcox and Carl Marcy, *Proposals for Changes in the United Nations* (Washington: Brookings Institution, 1955), p. 154.

28. Stanley Hoffmann, *Organizations Internationales et Pouvoirs Politiques Des Etats* (Paris: Librarie Armand Colin, 1954), p. 308.

29. *Ibid.*   30. *Ibid.*, p. 309

V

1. Leland M. Goodrich, "Regionalism and the UN", *Journal of International Affairs*, Spring, 149, Vol. III, p. 14. For a more detailed analysis of the development of specific regional groupings and their constitutional texts see Ruth C. Lawson, *International Regional Organizations* (New York: Frederick A. Praeger, Inc., 1962).

2. John Herz, *International Politics in the Atomic Age* (New York: Columbia University Press, 1959), pp. 96-108.

3. Ernst Haas, "Regional Integration and National Policy," *International Conciliation*, May, 1957, p. 381.

4. Cited by Ross N. Berkes, "NATO and the UN," *World Affairs Interpreter*, Summer, 1953, p. 160.

5. *Ibid.*, p. 162.   6. *Ibid.*, p. 164.

7. See the report of the Royal Institute of International Affairs Study Group *Collective Self-Defense in Southeast Asia* (London: Royal Institute of International Affairs 1956).

8. Harold and Margaret Sprout, *Foundation of International Politics* (New York: D. Van Nostrand Company, Inc., 1962), p. 630.

9. Haas, *op. cit.*, p. 388.

10. In assessing the effectiveness of CENTO, John C. Campbell asserts that "The Central Treaty Organization makes possible a certain amount of common planning in the northern tier. The members are anxious to build up their armies, and the United States is acting wisely in helping them. But CENTO does not in fact offer the means of defending the Middle East against a major Soviet attack, by reason of the weakness of its members, particularly Iran, and because of the absence of cooperation on the part of Iraq, the lost partner, and the Arab states . . . The conclusion to be drawn . . . is that there is little point in trying to plan and prepare for an organized defense of the Middle East in a general war against the Soviet Union . . . " *Defense of the Middle East* (New York: Harper and Brothers, 1960), p. 192.

11. See, for example, Werner Levi, *Fundamentals of World Organization* (Minneapolis: University of Minnesota Press, 1950), who asserts that the Soviet system is not a regional system since its members are not truly independent. p. 85.

12. Haas, *op. cit.*, p. 393.   13. *Ibid.*

14. Ernst Haas summarizes the changes that have occurred within the Soviet bloc in a recent article: ". . . integration was least successful when the Communist Party of the Soviet Union possessed an organizational monopoly over the process. The Stalin period witnessed a minimum of military cooperation, no joint economic planning, no exchange of information apart from the slavish imitation in eastern Europe of Soviet examples, and no successful value-sharing among fellow communists. Integration was a one-way process in which the aims of the European satellites were simply subordinated to those of the Soviet Union. The brittleness of the structure stood exposed in the fal of 1956 (with the Hungarian and Polish uprisings). Now . . . there is little central direction but paradoxically a good deal of practical integration . . . The more varied the centers of power in the bloc become . . . the more likely the emergence of some habits of continuous intra-bloc adjustment by teachniques not unlike those of Western Europe." "International Integration: The European and the Universal Process," *International Organization*, Summer, 1961, pp. 378-379. The recent ideological disputes between the Soviet Union, Communist China, and Albania reveal that the once monolitic bloc structure is undergoing revision at least with regard to the question of the future strategy and tactics of the world Communist movement, necessitating the type of adjustment to which Professor Haas refers.

15. In Western Europe the obsolescence of economic nationalism rested on " . . . the growing realization that standards of living can be advanced, economic well-being assured, and prosperous international trade maintained only through cooperative effort

in reducing the barriers to trade . . ." Norman J. Padelford, "Regional Organization and the United Nations," *International Organization,* Vol. VIII, 1954, p. 207.

16. Jan J. Schokking and Nels Anderson, "Observations on the European Integration Process," *Journal of Conflict Resolution,* December, 1960, pp. 385-386.

17. That economic integration rests on factors other than the security threat is emphasized by Schokking and Anderson, *op. cit.,* who argue that passage of the threat of war would have still left Europe harassed by the giant economic power of the United States and the Soviet Union. p. 359.

18. Professor Norman Padelford supports this view in asserting that "Conviction on the part of the government in Washington that Western Europe cannot resolve the economic and political ills which has afflicted it since World War II, save by economic integration, has been a driving force behind much American efforts to convince the governments of Europe that they should take further steps toward regional organization and unity." *op. cit.,* p. 208.

19. Professor Haas has convinently summarized the findings of *The Uniting of Europe* in "The Challenge of Regionalism," in Stanley Hoffmann, editor, *Contemporary Theory in International Relations* (New York: Prentice-Hall, 1960) . This quotation is found on p. 229.

20. *Ibid.*   21. *Ibid.,* p. 231.   22. *Ibid.,* p. 235.

23. Haas, "International Integration," *op. cit.,* pp. 375-376.

24. *Ibid.,* p. 378.

25. Lincoln Gordon, "Economic Regionalism Reconsidered," *World Politics,* January, 1961, p. 245.

26. Haas, *op. cit.,* p. 373.

27. Haas, "The Challenge of Regionalism," *op. cit.,* p. 232.

28. Schokking and Anderson, *op. cit.,* p. 387.

29. Guetzkow, *op. cit.,* p. 65.

30. Haas, "International Integration," *op. cit.,* pp. 366-367.

31. While EEC is essentially an economic agency, the European Assembly which services it and the other functional communities constitute an embryonic regional parliament some day to be elected by direct popular vote. Paul Henri-Spaak has asserted that nothing could be more political in fact that integrating the economics of the Six. Cited by Schokking and Anderson, *op. cit.,* p. 408.

32. Cited by Emile Benoit, *Europe at Sixes and Sevens* (New York: Columbia University Press, 1961), pp. 240-241.

33. Shokking and Anderson, *op. cit.,* assert that "It turned out that the High Authority . . . enjoyed more power on paper than in fact. However free it was from control by the Council of Ministers, it could not disregard the organ which represented the governments of the Community. Without its cooperation, the High Authority could not in full confidence go forward with its work of establishing common markets for coal and steel." p. 396.

34. William Diebold, *The Schuman Plan* (New York: Harper and Brothers, 1959), pp. 604-605.

35. For a detailed description of these agencies see PEP, *European Organizations* (London: George Allen & Unwin Ltd., 1959), pp. 295-317. See also Benoit, *op. cit.,* and the Summer 1961 Symposium on European Regional Communities in *Law and Contemporary Problems.*

36. PEP, *op. cit.,* p. 335. The same authors, however caution that "it is as yet

too soon to pass judgement on the adequacy of the powers given to the new institutions, the methods and procedures adopted by them, or the extent to which a 'community outlook' prevails." p. 308.

37. For an analysis of the problems of applying conclusions drawn from the experience of European integration to the non-Western areas see Haas, "International Integration," *op. cit.*, pp. 379-382.

38. Gordon, *op. cit.*, p. 246.

39. Haas, "The Challenge of Regionalism," *op. cit.*, pp. 238-239.

40. *Ideology and Foreign Affairs*, Study Prepared at the Request of the Committee on Foreign Relations, United States Senate, by the Center for International Affairs, Harvard University, January 17, 1960, pp. 71-72.

VI

1. On the general subject being discussed here see also *Regional Security and the United Nations,* a forthcoming publication of the Brookings Institution. For a European viewpoint see Romain Yakemtchouk, *L'O.N.U.—La Sécurité Régionale et le Probléme du Régionalisme,* (Paris: A. Pedone, 1955).

2. For a cogent analysis of the rationale of neutralism see George Liska, *Nations in Alliance* (Baltimore: Johns Hopkins Press, 1962), pp. 203-219.

3. *Ibid.*, p. 209.   4. *Ibid.*

5. Ernst Haas, "Regionalism, Functionalism, and Universal International Organization," *World Politic,* January, 1956, pp. 238-264.

6. *Ibid.*, p. 251.   7. *Ibid.*, p. 257   8. *Ibid.*, p. 240.

9. Though the United States has been a generous contributor of military aid to the member states of these coalitions, they lack the military integration and coordinated defense planning characteristic of NATO.

10. Ernst Haas, *Regional Integration and National Policy, op. cit.*, p. 397.

11. Professor Norman Graebner asserts that "the alliance's chief deterrent power has not been built on local military installations capable of resisting a conventional attack but on nuclear weapons and the means of conveying them to targets behind the Iron Curtain." "Alliances and Free World Security," *Current History,* April, 1960, p. 216.

12. Robert E. Osgood, "NATO: Problems of Security and Collaboration," *American Political Science Review,* March, 1960, p. 122. For comprehensive analysis of the politico-military-strategic aspects of the alliance see by the same author *NATO: The Entangling Alliance,* (Chicago: University of Chicago Press, 1961)

13. Robert E. Osgood, "Stabilizing the Military Environment," *American Political Science Review,"* March, 1961, p. 37.

14. *Problems and Trends in Atlantic Partnership,* Some Comments on the European Economic Community and NATO, Staff Study Prepared for the Committee on Foreign Relations, Senate, September 14, 1962, p. 33.

15. *Ibid.*, p. 34-34.

16. Liska, *op. cit.*, pp. 276-277.

17. An example of such assurances is contained in an article by McGeorge Bundy in *Foreign Affairs*: "Where and how the nuclear defenses of NATO should be deployed and engaged are, of course, important questions, but they are questions wholly subord-

inate to the reality that the whole strength of the United States . . . is engaged for
Europe's freedom . . ." October, 1962, p. 16.

18. Inis L. Claude, *Swords Into Plowshares: The Problems and Progress of International Organization, op. cit.,* pp. 121-122.

19. For a penetrating analysis of the motivations of the principal actors in the Suez crisis, see John Stoessinger, *The Might of Nations* (New York: Random House, 1961), pp. 129-136.

20. Haas, *op. cit.,* pp. 414-415.

21. Haas, "European and Universal Integration," *op. cit.,* p. 380.

22. *Ibid.,* p. 381.

23. Northwestern University, *The Organization of American States,* Study No. 3 prepared for the Committee on Foreign Relations, United States Senate, December 24, 1959, p. 216.

24. *Ibid.,* p. 217.   25. *Ibid.*   26. *Ibid.,* p. 221.

27. Philip B. Taylor, Jr., "The Guatemalan Affairs: A Critique of United States Foreign Policy," *American Political Science Review,* September, 1956, pp. 797, 805.

28. *Ibid.,* p. 805.

29. Reply of the Permanent Court of International Justice for advisory opinion on the Status of Eastern Carelia, July 23, 1923, cited by Claude, *op. cit.,* p. 234.

30. Although there is as yet no adequate discussion of this problem, the following sources are useful starting points: Robert Asher and associates, *The United Nations and the Promotion of Welfare* (Washington: Brookings Institution, 1957) and David L. Gordon, *Regional Approaches to Economic Development,* Paper prepared for delivery at the 1960 Annual Meeting of the American Political Science Association in New York.

31. Francis Wilcox and Carl Marcy, *op. cit.,* p. 88.

32. W. R. Malinowski, "Centralization and Decentralization in the United Nations Economic and Social Activities," *International Organization,* Summer, 1962, pp. 521-541.

33. "Issues before the Seventeenth General Assembly," *International Conciliation,* September, 1962, p. 86.   (cited in)

34. *Ibid.,* p. 89.   35. *Ibid.,* p. 90.   36. Gordon, *op. cit.,* p. 2.
37. *Ibid.,* p. 3.   38. *Ibid.,* pp. 3-4.

39. C. Wilfred Jenks, *The Common Law of Mankind* (New York: Frederick A. Praeger, Inc., 1958), p. 221.

40. *Ibid.,* p. 213.

41. Each of the specialized agencies is an independent legal entity with its own budget. secretariat, and administrative organization.   Though the agencies have entered into agreements with the United Nations as provided for by Article 63 of the Charter, these agreements do not involve the surrender of any powers and depend for their effectiveness on the voluntary harmonization of administrative and fiscal policies with the United Nations.   While the independence of these agencies from the United Nations has been the object of a good deal of criticism from public administration experts and others in recent years, a recent report of the Committee on Foreign Relations validly argued that the existence of an autonomous status " . . . has enabled many of them to carry on operations in spite of the cold war stalemate which has hampered United Nations operations in some fields."   Subcommittee on the United Nations Charter, Committee on Foreign Relations, United States Senate, *The United Nations and the Specialized Agencies,* July 25, 1955, p. 18.

42. On the other hand, it has been maintained that these nations are also suspicious to some extent of United Nations aid: "Even the UN and its specialized agencies, although their position in relation to the less developed countries differs substantially from that of individual aid-giving nation, suffers in some degree from this handicap. Inevitably they acquire most of their funds, their predilections and their personnel from the industrial countries and hence appear, to some extent, as agents of the latter." Gordon, *op. cit.*, p. 7.

43. Asher, *op. cit.*, pp. 98-99.   44. *Ibid.*, p. 101.

45. Northwestern University, *op. cit.*, p. 234.

46. For an analysis of some of the problems of what has been termed North-South integration see Gordon, *op. cit.*, pp. 11-14. In noting some of the economic difficulties of contemporary inter-regional cooperation, Professor Lincoln Gordon predicts the possibility of a major coffee war between Latin America and Africa if African states gain favorable access to European markets. "Economic Regionalism Reconsidered," *op. cit.*, p. 252. He argues that "the United States should press for general adherence to a policy of interregional non-discrimination, under which the industrially advanced groups would give equal access to food, raw material and manufactured goods from all underdeveloped areas, and the underdeveloped regions would to the extent that they were protecting infant industries protect them on a uniform basis . . . and offer to outsiders equal facilities for the sale of capital goods and for investments." *Ibid.*

47. Asher, *op. cit.*, p. 101.

48. Ruth Lawson, *International Regional Organizations* (New York: Frederick A. Praeger, Inc., 1962), p. vii.

49. Northwestern University, *op. cit.*, p. 234.

50. Stanley Hoffmann, "The Role of International Organization: Limits and Possibilities," *International Organization*, Vol. X, 1956, pp. 366-370.

51. *Ibid.*, p. 368.   52. *Ibid.*, p. 368-369.

53. *Issues before the Seventeenth General Assembly*, *op. cit.*, p. 135.

54. Cited in *Ibid.*, p. pp. 98-99.

55. Maxwell Graduate School of Citizenship and Public Affairs, Syracuse University, *The Operational Aspects of United States Foreign Policy*, A Study Prepared for the Committee on Foreign Relations, United States Senate, November 11, 1959, pp. 51-55.

56. *Ibid.*, p. 53.   57. *Ibid.*, p. 54.   58. *Ibid.*

59. *Ibid.*, p. 55.

60. *Issues before the Seventeenth General Assembly*, *op. cit.*, p. 126.

61. Center of International Studies, Massachusetts Institute of Technology, *Economic, Social and Political Change in the Underdeveloped Countries and Its Implications for the United States Policy*, A Study Prepared for the Committee on Foreign Relations, United States Senate, March 30, 1960, pp. 87-88.

63. Malinowski, *op. cit.*, p. 524.

64. *Ibid.*   65. *Ibid.*, pp. 531-537.   66. *Ibid.*, p. 540.

67. As cited in *Ibid.*, p. 536.   68. David Gordon, *op. cit.*, p. 15.

69. *Ibid.*, p. 2.

70. *Observations on the Operation of the Alliance for Progress: The First Six Months*, A Study Prepared for the Subcommittee on American Republic Affairs of the Committee on Foreign Relations, United States Senate, August 3, 1962, p. 10.

71. Robert Asher, Discussion of Paper by David Gordon, *op. cit.*, p. 4.

VII

1. J. M. Yepes, Les Regionaux Accords et le Droit International, *Recueil des Courts* 71 (1947), pp. 235, 240.

2. Pierre Vellas, *Le Regionalisme Internationale et L'Organisation des Nations Unies,* Paris, 1948, p. 62.

3. Gerard J. Mangone, *The Idea and Practice World Government* (New York: Columbia University Press, 1951), p. 55.

4. Haas, *Regional Integration and National Policy, op. cit.,* p. 438.

5. Yepes, *op. cit.,* p. 244.

6. The following section is based largely on Roger D. Masters, "A Multi-Bloc Model of the International System,'" *American Political Science Review,* December, 1961, pp. 780-798.

7. The term is borrowed from Professor Morton Kaplan. See his *System and Process In International Politics* (New York: John Wiley and Sons, 1957).

8. Commission to Study the Organization of Peace, *op. cit.,* p. 35.

9. Masters, *op. cit.,* p. 798.

10. *Ibid.,* p. 781.   11. *Ibid.,* pp. 783-787.   12. *Ibid.,* p. 789.

13. Especially when it is recognized that there is no provision for the possibility of a "balancer" in a system in which the vast majority of states are members of blocs.

14. John Herz, *International Politics in the Atomic Age* (New York: Columbia University Press, 1959), pp. 34-35.

15. Masters, *op. cit.,* p. 790.   16. *Ibid.,* p. 794.

17. Herz, *op. cit.,* pp. 182-183.   18. *Ibid.,* pp. 96-108.

19. Masters, *op. cit.,* footnote 38 pp. 785-786.

20. Herz, *op. cit.,* pp. 338-339.

21. *Ibid.,* pp. 309-310.

22. *Ibid.,* p. 302. A possible exception may be found on page 343 where Herz mentioned that the "territorial jurisdiction over individuals and groups included in the nation-state will be broken by diverse influence emanating from supraterritorial agencies." What these influences are and how they will operate is not described.

VIII

1. Bhoutros-Ghali, *op. cit.,* p. 230.

2. Harvey Wheeler, "The Role of Myth Systems in American-Soviet Relations," *Journal of Conflict Resolution, June,* 1960, pp. 171-184. See also Stoessinger, *op. cit.,* who argues that the "the two super-powers have struggled not only with each other, but with the images of each other. This divergence between image and reality has exacerbated the conflict enormously." p. 413 and ff.

3. Bhoutros-Ghali, *op. cit.,* p. 228.

4. Claude, *op. cit.,* p. 125.